Hawaii

D0268857

APA PUBLICATIONS

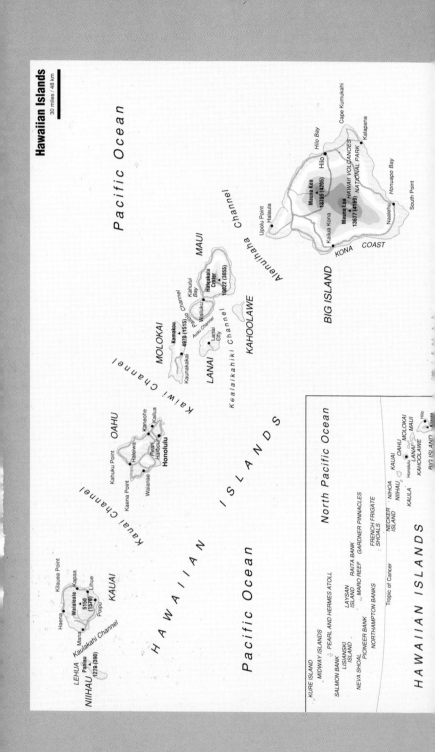

Hawaiian Islands

30 miles / 48 km

Pacific Ocean

Pacific Ocean

North Pacific Ocean

KAUAI
Haena Kilauea Point Kapaa
Waialeale 5150 (1570) Lihue
Maana Poipu
Kaulakahi Channel

NIIHAU
LEHUA Paniau 1279 (390)

Kauai Channel

OAHU
Kahuku Point
Haleiwa Kaneohe
Kaena Point Kailua
Waianae Pearl Harbor
Honolulu

Kaiwi Channel

MOLOKAI
Kaunakakai Kamakou 4970 (1515)

Pailolo Channel
Kahului Bay
MAUI
Wailuku Haleakala Crater 10022 (3055)
Lanai City
Auau Channel

LANAI

Kealaikahiki Channel

KAHOOLAWE

Alenuihaha Channel

BIG ISLAND
Upolu Point
Halaula
Hilo Bay
Hilo
Mauna Kea 13795 (4205)
HAWAII VOLCANOES NATIONAL PARK
Cape Kumukahi
Kalapana
Mauna Loa 13677 (4169)
Honuapo Bay
Kailua Kona
KONA COAST
Naalehu
South Point

H A W A I I A N I S L A N D S

HAWAIIAN ISLANDS

North Pacific Ocean

KURE ISLAND
MIDWAY ISLANDS

SALMON BANK ○ PEARL AND HERMES ATOLL

LISIANSKI ISLAND
LAYSAN ISLAND
NEVA SHOAL
PIONEER BANK
NORTHAMPTON BANKS
RAITA BANK
MARO REEF
GARDNER PINNACLES
FRENCH FRIGATE SHOALS
NECKER ISLAND

Tropic of Cancer

NIHOA · NIIHAU · KAUAI
OAHU
KAULA MOLOKAI
LANAI MAUI
KAHOOLAWE
Honolulu Hilo
BIG ISLAND

H A W A I I A N I S L A N D S

Dear Visitor!

Welcome to the Hawaiian islands, the world's oldest, longest and tallest island chain, and ironically its most remote, even with seven million visitors annually. Crowning these islands is Honolulu, a shiny city of nearly a million multi-racial people who speak a medley of languages. The cultural and ethnic brew is intoxicating; the islands' physical beauty even more so.

In these pages, Scott Rutherford, Insight's correspondent to Hawaii, has crafted itineraries that are perfect for a short stay. A selection of full- and half-day tours cover Oahu, the Big Island, Kauai and Maui. For those who have the luxury of time, there are day trips to the lesser-known, but no less intriguing, islands of Molokai and Lanai. Chapters on activities, eating out, shopping and nightlife, and a useful practical information section, complete this reader-friendly guide.

Scott Rutherford was first dispatched to Hawaii in 1985 on a book assignment. Unlike most travelers, he by-passed Oahu and went directly to Kauai's north shore, arriving under the turbid shroud of a midnight rain and jet lag. Hours later, a resplendent sunrise evaporated that shroud and the blue-green Hanalei Bay was revealed in all its glory. His seduction was repeated a few evenings later by a woman with a golden smile. The woman, as they've tended to do in Rutherford's nomadic wanderings, left. But Hawaii remained home for several years. Having scoured the most remote corners of the islands several times over, Rutherford is amply qualified to write this book. His suggestions are opinionated at times — sunsets are meant to be worshipped everyday like some cultish liturgy — but always insightful.

Hans Höfer
Publisher, Insight Guides

CONTENTS

Pages 2/3: the Hawaiian coastline is lush and inviting

*Pages 8/9:
a winter waverider
at Sunset Beach,
Oahu*

HISTORY & CULTURE

For such a small and idyllic place in the middle of a beautiful nowhere, Hawaii's history has been an almost non-stop struggle for dominance over land and values.

Everyone arriving in Hawaii has always *wanted* something from the islands. The first settlers from the Marquesas wanted refuge. Tahitians wanted what the early Marquesians had, namely, everything. Tribal chiefs fought among themselves for pieces of the islands. A more powerful chief wanted not just one island, but *all* of them. Whalers and missionaries bickered over bodies and souls. Sugar and pineapple barons wanted land and then more land. Twentieth century newcomers wanted – and still do – a parcel of paradise, if not all of it. It's never-ending, this *wanting* of Hawaii. Each new arrival steps on the toes of those who came before, usurping the place of those who feel they are the rightful heirs to the land. But in the beginning, there was nobody.

Natural History

Hawaii is like some student's science project explaining island development and decay, with islands at various evolutionary stages all lined up in chronological order. Hop along the 1,500-mile (2,400-km) long Hawaiian chain and one follows the geological history of the islands, indeed, of any island.

Lava confronts the ocean, Big Island

Hawaii sits in the middle of a tectonic plate, far from the plate's edges and possible collisions with nearby plates. The area known as the Pacific Rim is defined by these colliding plates; along this so-called rim of fire, lofty mountain ranges like the Andes are forced up and island archipelagos like Japan and Indonesia are created. Volcanoes and earthquakes come with the package.

But Hawaii is different. Tens of millions of years ago, magma from deep in the earth's mantle bled through a thin spot in the tectonic plate that present-day Hawaii sits on. The first Hawaiian island began growing, layering itself as a shield volcano with successive and reasonably sedate eruptions over time. It finally surfaced and became an island – actually a steep, immense mountain when measured from its base. The island's weight eventually sealed the thin spot, but the tectonic plate was, and still is, sliding northwest (perhaps four inches yearly). The hot spot burned new holes in the plate to create a successive chain of islands, and *voila...* the 132 Hawaiian islands and atolls. The city of Honolulu is 1,367 miles (2,190km) from Kure Atoll, the most northwest island of the state.

The youngest island – the Big Island – is smooth and rounded, typical of shield volcanoes. Follow the islands to the northwest where each successive island is older and more eroded – angular, lower and less massive.

The islands sat naked for a long time. Eventually, plant seeds borne by high winds, tides, or daring migratory birds took root. Insects and more birds followed. There are now 10,000 insect species alone in Hawaii, nearly all of them unique to the island. Each new species made itself a niche, and competition from similar species and the threat of enemies were almost non-existent. Many species evolved into less defensive species; plants, for example, lost their thorns or poisonous oils. The first two mammal species, the monk seal and the hoary bat, did little to upset the balance of nature. When people came, however, they brought plants and animals that have ecologically decimated Hawaii's indigenous species. As a result, little of Hawaii today is original.

Human History – Before the Europeans

Think of Hawaii, and among other things, one thinks of coconuts, banyans, banana trees, *ti* plants, bamboo, plumeria and orchids, papayas and mangoes, pineapples and taro. But none of these are Hawaiian. They were introduced by Polynesians and Europeans, along with mosquitoes, termites, fleas, cockroaches and ants, not to mention rats, dogs, pigs, and chickens. (Snakes never made it, although now and then an occasional stowaway is found in the wheel wells of incoming jumbo jets.)

The first people arrived around AD300, give or take some centuries, and probably accidentally at first, but later in continual migrations over several centuries. It is thought that they came from the Marquesas Islands, across 2,500 miles (4,023km) of open ocean in canoes. Seeking to escape domestic turmoil or population pressures, they navigated by stars and by literally reading the ocean and its contours. Originally violent and cannibalistic, the newcomers settled down over four or five centuries, becoming peaceful over time. Then the Tahitians arrived around 1100. Aggressive and wanting the islands for themselves, the Tahitians conquered and enslaved the Marquesians. Tahitian migrations continued for several centuries, then ebbed and stopped. Hawaii was once again isolated. A civilization coalesced, with social, political and economic hierarchies becoming well-defined: the royal *ali'i*, the *kahuna* – the spiritual and enlightened elite – and the *maka'ainana*, or commoners.

Life was not idyllic and peaceful. The majority of people – the commoners working the land – lived under feudal conditions defined by the strict law of *kapu* – the laws of forbidden things to do, eat, see, or walk upon. Violations, however well-intentioned, were punishable by immediate death. Added to this, tribal identities were now firmly entrenched, and with it, almost continual fighting.

The Arrival of the Europeans

There is speculation that Europeans – most likely the Spanish – might have visited Hawaii before Captain James Cook. But we now know that in January of 1778, Cook and his ships, the *Discovery* and the *Resolution*, skirted past Oahu before dropping anchor in Kauai's Waimea Bay. The Polynesian migrations had long ceased, and protected by geographical and cultural

A tatooed hula dancer

isolation, the *ali'i* and *kahuna* classes had established a secure power structure for themselves within their tribes. At the same time, there was constant conflict with the other tribes.

Cook's arrival upset the system in a number of ways. Most immediate was the introduction of disease to the islands; half his crew of 112 had venereal disease. Cook unsuccessfully tried to restrict his men's socializing with island women. Contrary to revisionist images of Western explorers, Cook was considered to be a decent, humane and benevolent man, fully aware, as his journals show, of the irreversible change his visits would bring throughout the Pacific.

Not only did the Hawaiians succumb to venereal disease, but also to common Western illnesses for which the Hawaiians had no immunity against. In the fifty years after Cook's arrival, the native population is estimated to have dropped from 300,000 to 60,000.

Cook's arrival on the Big Island – and his death there the following year – was witnessed by a young man. A careful observer of the Europeans and their weapons, Kamehameha – the lonely one –

was a quick student. He began his conquest of Hawaii a decade later, first with rival chiefs on the Big Island, then of the neighboring islands. Taught European battle tactics by Captain George Vancouver (who was on Cook's original voyage, as was Captain Bligh, later of the HMS *Bounty*), Kamehameha used a canoe-mounted cannon to conquer all the islands, save Kauai, which yielded to pragmaticism years later. What motivated Kamehameha is debatable. Some call him Napoleonic, while others prefer to think of him as a visionary. Whatever it was, Hawaii experienced continual peace during Kamehameha's rule.

Kamehameha's death in 1819 was followed almost immediately by the arrival of the first whaling vessels, the collapse of the *kapu* system (his favorite wife and son broke a *kapu* taboo by eating together), and the arrival of the New England missionaries.

Societies without anchors are vulnerable, and when the *kapu* system evaporated, a vacuum waited to be filled. The new missionaries obliged. Not only did they fill the spiritual vacuum, they completely destroyed all aspects of Hawaiian culture, like the hula, sacred *mele* chants, the native value system, and any connection at all with the Hawaiian past before 1820.

About the same time, Hawaii became an international whaling center, with hundreds of vessels dropping anchor in Hawaii every year. Whalers, expecting a lusty good time, and missionaries were often at odds; one whaling crew was so frustrated that they fired cannonballs at a preacher's new house in Lahaina.

Whaling died out, the whalers left, and the missionary families began to consolidate their power. Within a generation or two, their names – Bishop, Campbell, Cooke, Wilcox – became synonymous with land ownership and political power. But the names of power didn't stop with the missionaries.

The arrival of Captain Cook on Big Island

Hawaiian and Pidgin Words

No chance for us to learn Hawaiian in a short time. But there are a number of words used in daily conversation throughout the islands. Thanks to the early missionaries, Hawaiian has but 12 roman letters in its alphabet. Like Spanish, the a, e, i, o, and u vowels have only one pure sound; no lazy English vowel sounds. W confuses people: after i or e it is usually, but not always, pronounced as a v. At the start of the word, follow custom. Some Hawaiian words seem a little long, for example, humuhumunukunukuapua'a. Many long words use repeating structures. In the above word, which is a common trigger fish, humu and nuku each appear twice. So now, humu humu nuku nuku apu a'a is more manageable. But not all apparent repeating sounds are in fact that way. When in doubt, just ask. Good luck.

aloha: love, greetings, farewell
ali'i: royalty, chief
haole: outsider or foreigner, esp. Caucasian
kama'aina: local resident
keiki: child, boy or girl
kokua: help, assistance
lanai: porch, balcony
mahalo: thank you
malihini: newcomer
ohana: family
paniolo: cowboy
pau: finished

Pidgin

There's only one rule in the speaking or pronunciation of pidgin English: don't. You'll sound quite stupid, if not ridiculous; only a local raised in Hawaii can speak pidgin properly. But it's nice to understand some of what you might hear.

beef: fight or physical disagreement
brah: brother, friend
cockaroach: steal, rip off
da kine: the thing being talked about, or when you can't think of the right word
howzit: How are you?
mo' bettah: better, something good
no can: cannot
poi dog: hound dog of indeterminate origins, mutt
stink eye: a dirty look
talk story: conversation, chit chat

Businessmen and entrepreneurs replaced whalers, and they wanted land, not whales and women. The Hawaiian monarchy was pressured to recognize the idea of land *ownership*, not the traditional Hawaiian idea of land *use*, usually decided by the king. The Great Mahele of 1848 divided the land between the monarchy, the chiefs, and the people. The businessmen saw a certain future, and foreign ownership of land was approved two years later. The local people, still baffled by the idea of ownership, were taken for a penny.

Once land ownership became the law of the island, business and agricultural empires flourished. Sugar dominated the economy, along with export of natural resources like sandalwood to China, which was enthusiastically undertaken by the Hawaiian monarchy. In 1891, the new Queen Lili'uokalani became a business threat: she had turned reactionary by threatening to constitutionally strengthen native Hawaiian power. Two years later, a coup d'etat comprising businessmen overthrew the monarchy, and within hours, American troops landed on Hawaii.

A republic was declared, Sanford Dole was named president (his son would make pineapples famous), and six years later, Hawaii was part of American territory. The roster of powerful family names grew: Smart, Castle, Cooke, Baldwin, Alexander, Brewer. Some of these names combined forces, eventually known as an entity called the Big Five; for example, Castle & Cooke, and Alexander & Baldwin. The Big Five, along with

the Smarts' Parker Ranch, today own 22 percent of Hawaii – over a third of all private property in the state.

But as the agricultural concerns gained in power and size, they needed more workers. Chinese, Japanese, Europeans and Filipinos were imported as contract workers. Over the years, many of these people chose to make Hawaii home. They themselves became entrepreneurs, and the power balance began to shift.

People started to marry across racial lines, hardly common anywhere in the world then. One's identity was no longer a racial one so much as it was of a group, albeit a group still defined by ethnic traditions. Too, people began to think of themselves as *American* in some ways, and with that feeling the notion of power participation and shared decision making. The ruling families lost their oligarchical omnipotence. Statehood in 1958 and the economic power of the tourism industry made it irreversible.

Japan attacked Pearl Harbor on December 7, 1941, bringing both the United States and Hawaii into adulthood. Ironically, while thousands of Americans of Japanese ancestry (AJAs) on the mainland were imprisoned as security risks, few of the Japanese in Hawaii were persecuted, although the suspicion and rumor-mongering – in large part by mainlanders – was considerable. As a large portion of Hawaii's population was AJA, mass imprisonment was impractical. But equally important, if not more so, was that the other ethnic and cultural groups in Hawaii had no doubts about the loyalty of the AJAs. The Japanese-Americans were *kama'aina* (local residents), after all.

Some Social and Cultural Considerations

Simplifying a complex history involving numerous cultural and economic perspectives is dubious and risky. When one says *Hawaiian* today, who is one talking about? The racially-pure descendents of the early Tahitians – now numbering less than a thousand? Even that classification is questionable, given the sexual mingling that started the day Cook's ships dropped anchor in Hawaii. Or does one mean a person with the right attitude, a resident who has adopted to local ways rather than imposed outside ones? No one has a good answer, it seems, and neither do I.

Hawaii is often mentioned as an example of a truly-extraordinary co-existence of diverse cultural and ethnic interests. But racial and cultural prejudices do exist among the various groups. Human nature demands such. Rarely does it exist on an individual level; usually it's more a group thing. Cultural identity in Hawaii can be strong, almost clannish; yet on the individual level, Hawaii is very tolerant and diverse. Proof is the amazingly high percentage – nearly half – of inter-racial marriages. Also offered as proof, not so much empirical as observational, is the success of one of Hawaii's most popular entertainers, Frank De Lima. He takes group stereotypes and prejudices, and then rakes every group over the coals. De Lima is funny because his humor is based on the groups' idiosyncracies and eccentricities, and our acceptance of them. There are few places outside of Hawaii where a person could successfully make fun of the different racial groups as he does. What's clear, however, is that he respects them all.

Another example of the intermingling of races can be seen in Hawaii's food. As various ethnic groups arrived in the Hawaiian Islands throughout history, they brought with them their culinary traditions. Workers in the fields started tasting the unusual foods in each other's lunch boxes – Japanese teriyaki beef here, Korean kim chee there – and eventually they started borrowing ideas from each other. Today, many of Hawaii's eateries – be they high-end Euro-Asian restaurants or no-frills plate-lunch carry-outs – combine influences from the many gastronomical worlds of its people.

A local sentiment

Prejudicial problems exist in Hawaii, but they are mostly economically derived. Hawaii is, in many ways, becoming a place of haves and have-nots, where a service industry class is increasingly under the thumb, both politically and economically, of an affluent group of people sometimes new to Hawaii. Locals of all ethnic groups, having been pushed aside because of inflated housing costs, are forced to work service industry jobs that do not pay in proportion to the high cost of living.

The increasing economic disparity, which unfortunately often seems to follow along ethnic lines, is a conundrum that will test Hawaii's aloha in the years to come.

Historical Highlights

c. 300–500 AD Polynesians discover and settle uninhabited Hawaii.

c. 1100–1300 Tahitians arrive and overpower islands' earlier inhabitants.

c. 1400 Hawaiian society and culture develop, especially tribal and social class identities.

c. 1750 Kamehameha I born on the Big Island.

1778 Capt James Cook arrives at Waimea Bay, Kauai, with the British ships *Resolution* and *Discovery*.

1779 Capt Cook killed by Hawaiians at Kealakekua Bay, on the Big Island.

1790–95 Kamehameha I consolidates his power on the Big Island, then conquers Maui, Lanai, Molokai, and Oahu. Kauai submits by negotiation in 1810.

1803 Kamehameha makes Lahaina his capital.

1819 Kamehameha I dies. His wife and son abolish the kapu system.

1820 First Protestant missionaries arrive.

1835 First sugar plantation established in Kauai.

1840 Hawaii's first constitution introduced by Kamehameha III.

1842 United States recognizes the Kingdom of Hawaii.

1845 Hawaii's capital changed from Lahaina to Honolulu.

1848 Start of the 'Great Mahele', dividing land among royalty, commoners, government, and later, foreigners.

1852 First Chinese field workers arrive.

1866 First leprosy patients forced to Kalaupapa, on Molokai.

1868 First Japanese field workers arrive.

1872 Kamehameha V dies, ending Kamehameha dynasty.

1873 Father Damien arrives at Molokai leprosy colony, and dies in 1889 of leprosy.

1879 First Portuguese immigrants – and the ukulele – arrive.

1891 King Kalakaua dies, succeeded by Queen Lili'uokalani.

1893 Lili'uokalani is overthrown by American business interests. End of the monarchy.

1894 US recognizes the Republic of Hawaii. Sanford Dole is made president.

1898 US annexes Hawaii.

1900 US establishes the Territory of Hawaii.

1901 Waikiki's first real hotel, the Moana, opens. Pineapples introduced as a cash crop.

1912 Duke Kahanamoku, a surfing champion, wins a gold medal for swimming in the Olympics.

1927 First nonstop flight to Hawaii from North America.

1935 Radio broadcast of 'Hawaii Calls' begins from the Moana Hotel.

1941 Japan attacks Pearl Harbor on December 7.

1954 Japanese-Americans, the largest minority, dominate state legislature.

1959 Hawaii becomes the 50th American state. The first passenger jet lands.

1968 Surfing turns professional at Sunset Beach.

1974 George Ariyoshi becomes the first Japanese-American governor in US.

1976 A double-hulled canoe, the Hokule'a, leaves Hawaii for Tahiti using traditional navigation.

1982 Kauai is left devastated by Hurricane Iwa.

1983 Hawaii's population tops one million.

1986 The first ethnically-Hawaiian governor, John Waihee, takes office.

1990 Kilauea Volcano destroys Kalapana and surrounding homes.

1992 Hurricane Iniki slams Kauai, causing major damage, but slowly the island starts to rebuild.

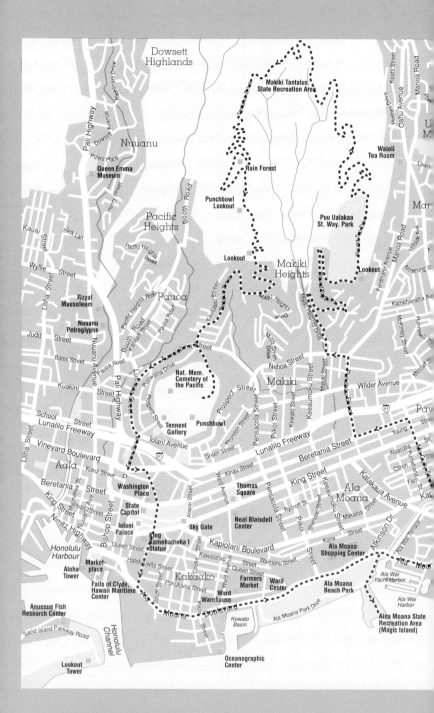

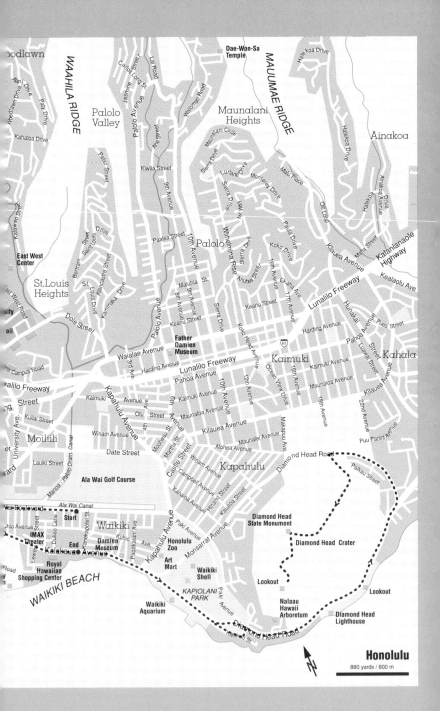

Oahu

A curse upon you should you never leave Waikiki while on Oahu. But in fact, a large percentage of visitors do exactly just that – they don't leave Waikiki except for the airport. It's certainly a blot on their reputation as travelers, for Oahu is one of the most beautiful islands anywhere in the ocean, whether or not one likes a big city on it. If the urban hum of Honolulu upsets any preconceptions of tropical paradise, on the other side of the mountain is terrain and life-style as rural as anywhere in the Hawaiian Islands.

But why dismiss Honolulu? It is one of the more pleasant cities anywhere – just the right size, a quirky hybrid of East and West, and with everything one needs to live well, and with enough nearby hiking trails, waterfalls, beaches and coral reefs to make any chamber of commerce whip itself into a lather. Yeah, I know, there is the traffic...

Our two-day itinerary covers the urban and the rural sides of Oahu. *Itinerary 1* starts with a perch atop Tantalus, overlooking the city and its setting. Then you descend right into the downtown district, exploring on foot its government, history, waterfront commerce, and business. An evening in Waikiki keeps the jet lag at bay. *Itinerary 2* circles the island, following a two-lane road along primal cliffs, exploding waves, and rolling fields of pineapple and sugar cane. It leads to the North Shore, better known as 'the country,' with landscapes so different from those on the Honolulu side that it could pass as one of the slower-paced neighboring islands.

The following three itineraries, shorter in duration, can be added to either of the first two itineraries, done separately, or strung together. *Itinerary 3* is a short loop around Oahu's stupendous southeast end, with super beaches and lookouts. This outing could take two hours or all day, depending on how much of a beach bum you turn into. The Bishop Museum (*Itinerary 4*) is something of a regional Smithsonian, where you could spend hours rambling around. The USS *Arizona* Memorial (*Itinerary 5*) is extremely popular, and requires three to four hours. Both the museum and memorial are centrally located.

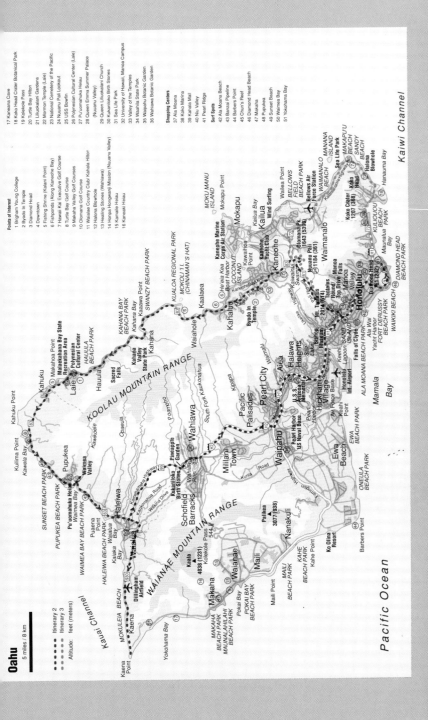

1. Honolulu and Waikiki Area

A first day in paradise – breakfast on the beach, followed by a ramble around Honolulu, the capital city. Lofty views, Hotel Street, Chinatown, the waterfront, America's only royal palace, parks and shopping, and, of course, Waikiki.

Outwit any pesky jet lag with a dawn ocean swim along Waikiki Beach, followed by a grand breakfast. This first Hawaiian breakfast must be proper – outside and embraced by the tropical morning. Trust me – there's no better way in Waikiki to baptize the day than from a table at **Orchids**, at the regal-like **Halekulani Hotel**, watching Diamond Head wake up. Alternatively, try an outside table at the **Banyan Veranda**, at the **Sheraton Moana-Surfrider** (c. 1901), Waikiki's first hotel.

Waikiki Beach from the Sheraton Waikiki

By car, follow Ala Wai Boulevard to McCully Street. The smooth waters of the Ala Wai Canal – built during the 1920s to empty the swamp now called Waikiki – ripple gently during outrigger canoe club practices. Follow McCully, then take a left into South Beretania Street, just before McCully arches into an overpass. Make a right into Punahou Street, but before it begins climbing into Manoa Valley, turn left into Nehoa Street, then right into Makiki Street.

Round Top Drive spirals upwards through a residential area, breaking out at a lookout with prime vistas towards Diamond Head and Waikiki. **Diamond Head** is a tuff cone, popping up about 150,000 years ago through the coral reef in a set of violent steam explosions. The ocean side of Diamond Head, arching upward, is higher because the northeast trade winds deposited more ash there. Directly below you, the lush and wet **Manoa Valley** opens from the Ko'olau Mountains; the 20,000-student University of Hawaii campus sprawls at the valley's mouth.

The road climbs further up **Tantalus** to **Pu'u'ualaka'a State Wayside Park**, nice for a short walk and still another stupendous view, this time extending from left of Diamond Head to Ewa. Notice that what you see is mostly flat, including downtown Hon-

National Memorial Cemetery, Punchbowl Crater

olulu. This is what geologists call a coral bench, formed when the sea level was 25ft (7½m) higher.

Continue up Tantalus through deep and lush rain forest, circling around and descending into **Punchbowl Crater**. Inside this tuff cone is the **National Memorial Cemetery of the Pacific**. The Hawaiian name for Punchbowl is Puowaina – hill of sacrifice, which it was in fact long ago.

Zigzag from Queen Emma Street to Vineyard Boulevard to Punchbowl Street. It's time for a walk. Suggested parking: left on King Street from Punchbowl, bearing left at the signal on Alapai Street and back again towards the mountains. Just before the Beretania Street signal is a nearly-camouflaged public lot; quarters are needed for the hungry 3-hour meter.

Find the **State Capitol Building**, with its tall slender pillars lifting the building above an open courtyard. On Beretania Street side

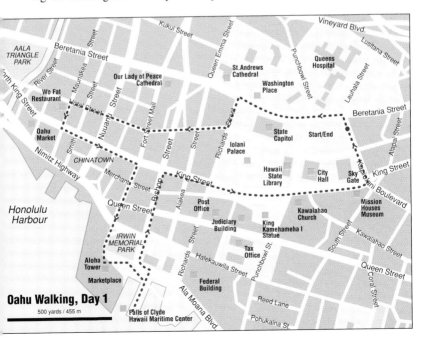

Oahu Walking, Day 1

500 yards / 455 m

is a bronze **statue of Father Damien**, priest to the Molokai leprosy colony. It faces **Washington Place**, built in 1846 from coral stone and now home to Hawaii's governor. From here, walk down Richards Street, then right onto Hotel Street.

Hotel Street was once a rowdy strip, a true port-of-call when sailors on liberty swarmed its sidewalks. It is difficult to imagine the rumpus of those seedy ol' days at this end, recently tidied up by urban renewal. Proceed down Hotel Street and into Chinatown.

Maunakea Marketplace

Despite burning down twice – in 1886, and again in 1900 to fight a bubonic plague epidemic – Chinatown is thick with old buildings, the stand-out being **Wo Fat**, a gaudy pink building and landmark Chinese cafe built in 1936. At Maunakea Street is **Maunakea Marketplace**, a cluster of stores and restaurants marked by a clock tower with Chinese numbers.

Left down Maunakea Street, then left on King Street, all the while poking through vegetable stalls, acupuncture clinics, herbalists, noodle factories, antique stores and hole-in-the-wall eateries.

Nu'uanu Avenue cuts across both King and Hotel Streets, and is noted for its quality art galleries.

Follow the **Fort Street Mall** straight down to the waterfront. Since 1926, the 184-ft (56-m) **Aloha Tower** has been the polestar of Honolulu's waterfront. The tower once greeted tourists arriving by boat, as did long waits in the cavernous processing area at the tower's base. Now it presides over **Aloha Tower Marketplace**, a new complex of shops and restaurants.

From the tower, it's five minutes to the **Falls of Clyde**, built in 1878 and used as a passenger ship between Honolulu and San Francisco. Definitely visit the **Hawaii Maritime Center**, with eclectic and informative displays, from whales to surfboards to ancient canoes.

Bishop Street leads back downtown, dominated by banks and corporate loftiness. Turn right on King Street to the **King Kamehameha I statue** – look for the flock of tourists. Don't be fooled by substitutions. This is a duplicate; the original statue stands on the Big Island. Commissioned to celebrate the centennial of Captain Cook's arrival in Hawaii, the original sank near the Falkland Islands en route from Europe. A duplicate was cast, and the original later recovered.

Opposite the monument is **Iolani Palace**, completed in 1882 by King Kalakaua after his European travels. From 1893 until 1969, after the monarchy's fall, the palace was the capitol building for the republic, territory, and finally the state.

Further down King Street are the **Mission Houses Museum** and **Kawaiahao Church**. The restored homes portray missionary life in the early 1800s; Kawaiahao Church was built in 1842 of coral cut from ocean reefs.

Behind the tall dull-grey municipal building across King Street is the park-

Aloha Tower

Ala Moana Center

ing garage. On the way, state law requires you to lay down underneath the **Sky Gate** sculpture, by Isamu Noguchi, and stare at the clouds.

By car, loop back around to Punchbowl Street and continue to Ala Moana Boulevard. Follow Ala Moana towards Waikiki, passing a succession of shopping centers: **Ward Warehouse**, casual with a wide mix of stores; **Ward Center**, upscale shopping and a number of deli-like places and popular restaurants; **Ala Moana Shopping Center**, the *ali'i* of Hawaii shopping centers, still growing and selling anything from plate lunches to unpronounceable Italian designer shoes.

Opposite Ala Moana Shopping Center is **Ala Moana Beach Park** and **Aina Moana State Recreation Area** (locals call Aina Moana 'Magic Island'). This is a wonderful place, a cultural theater of people at play. Walk out to the end of Magic Island for mesmerizing views of the yacht harbor, Waikiki, and Diamond Head. The late afternoon light casts a special atmospheric magic here.

Waikiki, a place to love and hate at the same time. Somehow it all works – the hotels, condominiums, shopping arcades, restaurants, movie theaters and the beach. And even more, it's got the best people-watching anywhere, with resplendent sunsets to boot. Five minutes by foot towards Diamond Head is the 200-plus-acre (69-ha) **Kapiolani Park**, embracing a zoo, aquarium, weekend art festivals, the perpetual **Kodak Hula Show**, an outdoor concert venue (**Waikiki Shell**) and plenty of open space for playing.

Imagine the view atop Diamond Head. Drive around Diamond Head, past the lighthouse and bronzed surfers in the water below,

Waikiki's Kalakaua Avenue

Banyan Courtyard, Moana Hotel

and drive straight into the crater from around back. A trail and stairs lead to the 761-ft (232-m) summit.

Eventually sunset beckons you to settle down. Nearly anywhere in Waikiki is good, from Diamond Head's summit to the arc of beaches below. For a proper drink and *pupus* with sunset, return to your breakfast spot at either the Halekulani or the Sheraton Moana-Surfrider. The Halekulani is best, I think, especially with a dinner at either the **Orchids** or **La Mer** restaurants. After sunset, try the **Parc Cafe** at the Waikiki Parc Hotel for its small but beautifully-prepared buffet with some delightful surprises, or stop by **Restaurant Suntory** at the Royal Hawaiian Shopping Center for the best sushi in Waikiki.

Wandering along Waikiki's **Kalakaua Avenue** at twilight is a wonderful experience. Impulsively as it sprouted from the swamp, impulsively is the manner Waikiki should be explored. Detailed Waikiki walking itineraries always fail dismally. But some recommendations: the **Historical Room** of the Sheraton Moana-Surfrider, with a collection of memorabilia from the hotel's rich past; the sunset **torchlighting ceremony** at the Diamond Head-end of Waikiki Beach, across from the Hyatt Regency; the **Royal Hawaiian Shopping Center** for traditional shopping, and the **International Marketplace** for an outdoor bazaar where bargaining is *de rigeur*; a table right next to the beach at the **Mai Tai Bar** (a duo strolls and sings island songs while bikinis parade on the sand) at the Royal Hawaiian Hotel, the legendary 'pink palace' built in 1927 along Moorish-Spanish lines; the **Hawaii IMAX Theater** for its staggering wide screen film about Hawaii; or the **beach** itself – quite safe at night – for a selection of evening entertainment, from gaudy but entertaining hotel Polynesian revues to intimate dining by the sea.

2. Island Circle – Windward and North Shores

A circular drive around Hawaii's most underappreciated island. See the world's most famous surfing area and a sacrificial heiau, then enjoy an evening among the stars, both literally and figuratively.

Statistics show that a good number of visitors confine their hearts and minds to the Waikiki area. So perhaps you should treat this itinerary as an escape. There's an island to drive around today, a simply beautiful island, mostly unappreciated. From Honolulu, tunnel through the Ko'olau Mountains, popping out on the windward side. There are two alternatives: the Likelike Highway, or the **Pali Highway**. Take the latter. Seconds after getting on the Pali from the H1 freeway, look out on your right for the **Honpa Hongwanji Mission**, a Buddhist temple impossible to miss. Beyond, the highway climbs steadily up **Nu'uanu Valley**.

Just before the top and the first of two short tunnels, pull off for **Nu'uanu Pali State Park**. The Ko'olau Range is the remnant of Oahu's younger of two extinct volcanos. The Honolulu side is the exte-

Honpa Hongwanji Mission

rior slope, gradual and corrugated with valleys. The windward side is the crater's interior, with cliffs rising up to 3,000ft (915m). Looking windward from the Pali overlook, **Kane'ohe** is left, **Kailua** is right and near the old volcano's eruptive center. The Lost Continent-looking spire across the way is the 1,643-ft (501-m) Olomana Peak, a stubborn caldera dike.

In 1795, during his Oahu conquest, Kamehameha I elbowed a group of defending warriors right over the cliff near the lookout. Ponder over that while descending towards Kailua the slow and safe way. At the bottom is a signal. Don't go straight, which leads to Kailua or southeast Oahu (see *Itinerary 3*). Rather, turn left on Route 83 and proceed through Kane'ohe, which has nothing to offer you today except **Byodo-In**, in the Valley of the Temples along Route 83. It's a beautiful replica of a temple in Japan; this one was built in 1968 to commemorate the centennial of Hawaii's first Japanese immigrants.

Stay on Route 83 northwards, snuggling the shoreline through primal-looking terrain. The drive is rural and quiet, with several pleasant stops along the way. **Kualoa Regional Park**, with a sensational beach and full facilities, is opposite **Chinaman's Hat**, properly called Mokoli'i. **Kahana Bay Beach Park**, backed by the cool rain forest of **Kahana Valley State Park**, is a tranquil stop for a picnic or an earnest snooze beneath whispering ironwood trees. Another excellent alternative further is **Malaekahana Bay State Recreation Area**, with good snorkeling and gentle waters.

You've seen the ubiquitous advertisements, now see the real thing (well, maybe): the **Polynesian Cultural Center**, owned and operated by the Mormon church. Clearly, many visitors don't mind the high price and sanitized theme-park milieu with its somewhat-Disneyland depiction of Oceanic cultures. Look at the tour bus parking lot and decide for yourself. I'll wait at the beach.

Kahuku is a quiet sugar town with two fun stops for a meal. First is **Ahi's**, serving up daily fresh seafood specials at bargain prices; look for its sign on top of the rusted-out truck by the side of the highway. Second is a roadside stand outside Kahuku selling shrimp and prawns, cultivated in the aquaculture ponds.

Crest Oahu's northern tip. Wind generators spin atop the hills on the left; nearby, the luxurious **Turtle Bay Hilton** nearly straddles the ocean. Its remote and quiet location speaks for itself. Due north is Alaska.

And now the **North Shore**, surf capital of known galaxy. Somewhere along 2-mile (3-km) long **Sunset Beach** is the infamous Banzai Pipeline. It's not marked, but scores of surfers coasting along the road know *exactly* where it is. Ask. If it's summertime, you'll wonder what the fuss is all about, as there's probably hardly a ripple, much less a wave, in sight. Come back in winter when waves reach 30ft (9m), even higher to the west.

Even more radical waves break at **Waimea Bay**. But just before Waimea, turn left at the Foodland grocery store, climbing the road to the **Pu'uomahuka Heiau** turnoff. This is the largest heiau, a large open-air temple, on Oahu. One can only hope that the view mellowed the misery of sacrificial victims in 1792, among them some hapless British sailors.

Behind Waimea Bay and the beach, a road leads to **Waimea Val-**

Refreshingly different North Shore

Pu'uomahuka Heiau

ley, an archeologically important site and nature preserve. It's a private park endeavoring to preserve and share Hawaii's flora, fauna, culture and history.

Head for **Hale'iwa**, the North Shore's center for local commerce and tourism. On weekends, heavy traffic makes a North Shore drive slow. Get out of the car if the traffic gets to you: there are plenty of places to shop. For the hungry: fish and ocean views at **Jameson's by the Sea**; local atmosphere and hearty meals at **Cafe Haleiwa**, especially for breakfasts that are famous island-wide; coffee, pastries and deli meals at **Coffee Gallery**, tucked away in the North Shore Marketplace, south of town.

An option: Continue along the coast to Mokule'ia Beach and Dillingham Airfield for exhilarating **glider rides**, or to the end of the road for an hour-long walk to **Ka'ena Point**, Oahu's western tip. In winter, 50-ft (15-m) high waves explode off-shore. It's believed that the spirits of the dead come here to depart earth, so watch your step.

From Hale'iwa, proceed along Route 99 south, inland through a broad valley between the Ko'olau and Wai'anae mountains. Fields of sugar cane and pineapple blanket the valley's red soil. Forget the Dole Pineapple Pavilion tourist trap on the left; no bargains on pineapples or juice, not even a lousy sample. But down the road, right at the intersection with Route 801, the dignified self-guiding **Del Monte pineapple garden** is interesting. Then follow the intersection's left fork a bit to a signal: left leads to Whitmore Village and right empties into a field of pineapple plants, where there is a grove of tall trees. Here you'll find the **Kukaniloko Birth Stones**, marked with petroglyphs and used by *ali'i* for giving birth.

Interstate H2 empties you onto Interstate H1 – towards Honolulu – right above **Pearl Harbor**. Consider stopping at the USS Arizona Memorial (see *Itinerary 5*) here. Interstate H1 also passes the Bishop Museum (see *Itinerary 4*).

Hit the beach or park, or return to the hotel. Rest up, freshen up, and then saddle up again. Drive around the front of Diamond Head to the **Kahala Mandarin Oriental**, noting some of the jillion-dollar estates along Kahala Avenue. Opened in 1964 as the Kahala Hilton, the hotel has been renovated to the tune of millions of dollars and continues to be a peerless and serene retreat, as international statesmen in transit and celebrities in hiding know well. A small beach fronts the hotel; this is where Kamehameha's war canoes landed nearby during his Oahu conquest. Feel the ocean breeze bring in the dusk, then get all romantic at the hotel's cosy **Hoku Restaurant**. Head back to Waikiki for one of the shows on the strip: the venerable Don Ho show in a more intimate and successful showroom than in years past; the irreverent Frank DeLima, who has a way of keeping us laughing at ourselves; the Broadway song-and-dance of the Society of Seven, the longest-running act in Waikiki; or a cozy spot under the stars of Waikiki Beach, where you can make your own beautiful music...

The sacred Kukaniloko Birth Stones

Hanauma Bay

3. Southeast Oahu Loop

A short trip around Oahu's southeast tip, which has some of the island's best beaches and best views. Can be driven in a couple hours, or extended to half a day with beach time.

It's a perplexing riddle why more visitors don't get out of Waikiki more often, for within half an hour are great beaches and scenery.

From Waikiki, drive around the tip of Diamond Head and along Kahala Avenue to a left at Hunakai Street, then right on Kilauea Avenue, past the Kahala Shopping Mall to the H1 Interstate, which terminates here. Turn right onto the Kalanianaole Highway, heading east. (Don't start this excursion in late afternoon, as rush hour traffic goes in the same direction.)

After several bedroom suburbs, the road climbs up and left. At the crest on the right is the road down to **Hanauma Bay**. It's a popular place with visitors, to the extent that it is now overused and on the threshold of ecological degradation. The state has had to restrict tour bus access and initiate a small entrance fee, and few locals visit it because of the intense crowds – as many as 10,000 people visit the bay daily. I strongly advise admiring it from up on top. There's a huge ocean around Oahu with lots of other places to play. *Let Hanauma Bay rest.*

The coast beyond Hanauma Bay is rugged, sculpted, and dramatic – testimony to the ocean's erosive power on the islands. The **Halona Blowhole** – where water is forced up geyser-like through a hole in the basalt when the incoming sea swell pushes up through its underwater entrance – is popular with the tour bus circuit. Just beyond, the road flattens out. That big beach is **Sandy Beach**, one of Oahu's most popular beaches. It's also a dangerous beach at times; the unique conditions that make it a superb board and body surfing place make it tricky for the swimmer. No joke: Sandy Beach

Southeast coast, Oahu

is a prime source of broken vertebrae in Hawaii. On the other hand, sometimes it's perfect for swimming. Before going in the water, check with the lifeguards.

The next stop is at the top of the **Makapu'u Lookout**. It's easy to zip right past the overlook when cresting the top as the view is a stunner. Looking straight up Oahu's windward coast, the lookout is one of Hawaii's best. For even better views, the **Makapu'u Lighthouse** stands tall on the top of the point. The one-mile climb up Lighthouse Road leads to lighthouse lookouts with panoramic views of mountains and sea, turtles and winter whales, islands and beaches. No restrooms, no food concession, not even that many other people. Just you and nature. **Makapu'u Beach** is known for its beautiful, but sometimes brutal, bodysurfing waves. Across from Makapu'u is **Sea Life Park**, with its sea life exhibits and porpoise shows.

The road bobs and dips towards Waimanalo, a very Hawaiian town known for its sumo wrestlers and rodeos, and for **Waimanalo Beach**, one of the longest and nicest white sand beaches anywhere. It's nearly empty on weekdays, but it's not exactly a paradise for naive visitors. Play it safe and lock the car before hitting the beautiful beach.

There's often a roadside stand in Waimanalo, selling home-grown corn on the cob. If you're cooking your own food at night, pick some up; it's bound to taste fresher than anything you find in the supermarkets. Continue past Olomana Peak on the left to the intersection with Route 61. Right leads to the town of Kailua. Left on Route 61 returns us to Honolulu. Just before it starts climbing to Nu'uanu Pali, a junction to Route 83 connects us with *Itinerary 2*, continuing north along the coast.

Popular Sandy Beach

4. Bishop Museum

A world-class museum and scientific institution. It's no simple boast to call the Bishop Museum the Pacific's equal to the Smithsonian. Highly recommended.

The Bishop Museum is a regional museum and research institute on par with the Smithsonian Institution in Washington, D.C. And like the Smithsonian, hours and hours can be spent exploring the Bishop. For this reason, I've recommended it as a separate option rather than trying to squeeze it into another full itinerary.

Founded in 1889 by Charles Reed Bishop, the museum was originally built as a memorial to his wife – the last direct descendant of the Kamehameha dynasty, Princess Bernice Pauahi. Her family heirlooms were the museum's first holdings, but in the 100 years since, the collection has expanded to comprise Oceania's finest specimens, both natural and human-made. Its collection is comprehensive and even overwhelming: some 200,000 Hawaiian and Pacific artifacts; 6,000,000 shells; 250,000 plant specimens; and 13,500,000 insect specimens.

The Bishop Museum supports and coordinates archeological and sociological research throughout the Pacific. Only a small portion of both this and its full collection is on display. Nonetheless, the displays are formidable, especially in the Hawaiian Hall. Other visitor possibilities include craft demonstrations, a planetarium, library and archives, and Shop Pacifica, a great gift shop for both browsing and buying.

Bishop Museum
State Museum of Natural & Cultural History
1525 Bernice Street, Honolulu 96817
Tel: 847 3511
Open 9am to 5pm daily. The admission fee includes entry to the Planetarium shows at 11am and 2pm, Friday and Saturday evenings at 7pm; reservations required for evening shows.

Bishop's Museum's Hawaiian Hall

5. USS Arizona Memorial and USS Bowfin Museum

Take a boat out to the memorial that stands over the sunken hull of the USS Arizona. Next door, walk through an authentic WWII submarine. Plan on three to four hours for both.

The USS **Arizona** needs little introduction. The memorial commemorates the December 7 1941 Japanese attack on Pearl Harbor. Over a thousand sailors died on the *Arizona*, when a series of Japanese torpedoes and aerial bombs sank the battleship. The remains of many are still entombed in the hull visible from the memorial. The memorial itself has three sections: the entry and assembly area; a ceremonial and observation area; and the shrine with the engraved names of those killed.

Pearl Harbor orientation

Often there is a wait of one to three hours for your turn to take the launch to the memorial. A film, visitor center, and bookstore easily help pass the time. The 20-minute documentary film about the attack is pleasantly free from jingoism and patriotic melodrama. The memorial program itself takes about 75 minutes. The *Arizona* Memorial and visitor center is operated and maintained by the US National Park Service, in cooperation with the US Navy.

Literally next door to the *Arizona* visitor center is the privately-owned USS **Bowfin Submarine Museum and Park**, five minutes away by foot and highly recommended. A genuine diesel-electric WWII submarine, the *Bowfin* was credited with sinking 44 ships during its nine patrols. It has since been refurbished to near-perfect condition. A walk through the submarine is really quite interesting. A huge museum traces submarine history from WWI to the nuclear submarine age.

USS Arizona Memorial
1 Arizona Memorial Place, Honolulu 96818
Tel: 422 0561
Open daily 7.30am to 5pm. No admission fee. The last program begins at 3pm. No reservations are accepted; it's first come, first served.

USS Bowfin Submarine Museum & Park
11 Arizona Memorial Drive, Honolulu 96818
Tel: 423 1341
Open daily 8am to 5pm. Admission fee for submarine and museum. For safety reasons, children under four are not allowed on the *Bowfin*, but they are most welcome in the museum.

The Bowfin conning tower

Hawaii the Big Island

The Big Island, just as promised... Twice as big as all the other Hawaiian islands combined. The youngest of the Hawaiian islands, the Big Island is actually just the above-water tip of the planet's biggest mountain, Mauna Loa, and its tallest mountain, Mauna Kea – measured from their bases. And the island still grows. Two active volcanoes punctuate the island, and a new subterranean island gestates 20 miles (32km) offshore.

Of all the Hawaiian islands, the Big Island is the most accessible for ancient Hawaiian history: temples, footpaths, petroglyphs and villages are numerous. Indeed, the Big Island was historically pivotal: it was the first landfall of venturing Polynesians from Tahiti, the last landfall of adventurous Captain Cook from England, and the point of departure for the conquest and unification of all Hawaii by Kamehameha I. Hilo, the state's largest city outside

Kohala Mountains, cool and casual

Oahu, hardly seems metropolitan, fortunately, but it's usually ignored by the visitor, unfortunately – Kona and Kohala get all the attention and most of the sunshine.

The Big Island is small enough to drive around in a day, but big enough to make the journey thoroughly unsatisfying. Just as you wouldn't try 15 European cities in 10 days, don't try the Big Island in one.

While the full-day tours (see *Itineraries 6* and *7*) itinerary pivot on a night or two in South Kohala or Kona, the dry and sunny side where most hotels are located, try to extend one of the shorter options (see *Itineraries 8* and *9*) and stay the second night in Hilo or Volcano, 30 minutes from one another. Save driving time and fly out of Hilo instead of Kona. Hilo and Hawaii Volcanoes National Park are separate options that can be added to the full-day itineraries if you're presed for time: Hilo to *Itinerary 6* and the park to *Itinerary 7*. Wet as it is, Hilo is one of my favorite parts of Hawaii simply because it's comfortable just being itself.

South Kohala's upmarket Mauna Lani Hotel

6. Kohala and Kona

Drive to the northern tip: a sacred temple, a king's birthplace, a commoners' fishing village. Cowboy country. The west coast: museum-quality art and classy resorts, petroglyphs, royal fishponds. Downtown Kona and a sunset.

Daybreak. Clear the mind with a glass of freshly-squeezed orange juice. Unfold the map and trace Route 19 north along the Big Island's western coast to North Kohala. If you've decided to add the Hilo option (see *Itinerary 8*) for a long day, finish the juice and hit the road. Otherwise, sure, order another glass.

From Kona, it's an extra 30-minute drive than from the Kohala resorts. The highway traverses miles of lava flows, most recently from 1859. Just north of the Keahole-Kona airport, the exclusive and uniquely reactionary **Kona Village Resort** (no televisions, telephones, or air conditioning amidst otherwise luxurious pampering) nestles down on the coast, where Hawaii's best luau fires up on Friday nights. In contrast, next door is the new and very upscale **Four Seasons Hualalai**. Further along, North Kona yields to South Kohala and a string of resorts and golf courses.

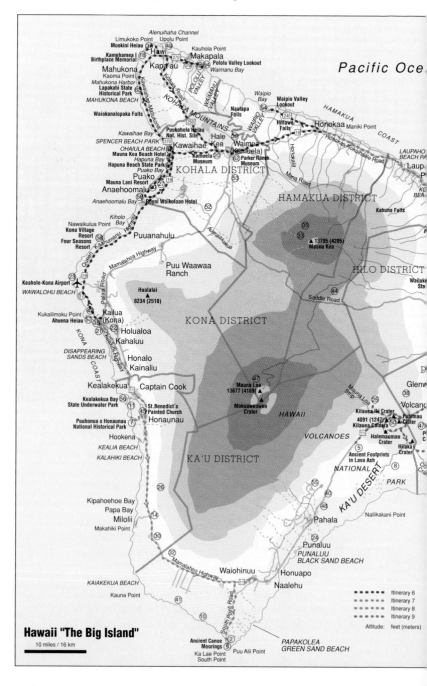

Hawaii "The Big Island"

10 miles / 16 km

Itinerary 6
Itinerary 7
Itinerary 8
Itinerary 9

Altitude: feet (meters)

At the junction leading to North Kohala's west coast, stop at the **Pu'ukohola Heiau**, a national historic site. Dedicated to the war god, it was built by Kamehameha I in 1791.

Follow Route 270 past Kawaihae, a utilitarian commercial port and the site where Kamehameha's war canoes set off for conquest. **Lapakahi State Historical Park** is a look back into the past of 600 years ago; in the early morning coolness it's a satisfying self-guiding walk through this stone ghost town of a commoners' fishing village.

The road ascends inland over increasingly green hills. Take the **Upolu Point** turnoff, where a modest straight-arrow road leads (after a left at the airstrip) to a passable – except when wet – dirt road to the **Mo'okini Heiau**, a temple still maintained by a kahuna from the Mo'okini family, heiau guardians for perhaps a thousand years. The heiau was built around AD480. Nearby is **Kamehameha's Birthplace**, c. 1752. Signs mark both the heiau and the birthplace. Linger here for an hour, if not an eternity.

The main road takes you through Hawi, a one-time sugar boom town, and on to Kapa'au, where the original **King Kamehameha statue** stands before the unassuming civic center. Refuel with a tofu burger and some wicked chocolate pie from **Don's Family Deli** on the Akonipule Highway, the main route through Kapa'au.

At the road's end is the **Pololu Valley Lookout**, teasing visitors with peeks

Points of Interest
1 Akaka Falls State Park
2 Ancient Canoe Moorings, Ka Lae
3 Kalamanu
4 Kalapana
5 Mauna Iki Footprints
6 Boiling Pots
7 Puuhonua o Honaunau National Historical Park
8 Hawaii Volcanoes National Park
9 Heiau o Kalalea
10 Heiau o Molilele
11 Hikiau Heiau State Monument
12 Hilo Country Club
13 Hilo International Airport
14 Hoopuloa Church Monument
15 Hulihee Palace, Mokuaikaua Church
16 Kalahikiola Church
17 Kaloko Fishpond
18 Kamehameha I Birthplace
19 Kamehameha I Statue
20 Kamuela Museum
21 Kauakaiakaola Heiau
22 Keauhou-Kona Golf Course
23 Keahole-Kona Airport
24 Kane'ele 'ele Heiau
25 Kipuku Puaulu Bird Park
26 Koa Mill
27 Puako petroglyphs
28 Liliuokalani Gardens, Suisan Fish Market
29 Lyman Museum and Mission House
30 Macadamia Nut Farms
31 Mahinaakaka Heiau
32 Manuka State Park
33 Mauna Kea
34 Mauna Kea Beach Hotel
35 Mauna Kea Observatory
36 Mauna Loa
37 Mookini Heiau (480 A.D.)
38 Olaa Rain Forest
39 Parker Ranch Headquarters
40 Kapapala
41 Pohue Bay
42 Puhina o Lono Heiau
43 Puukohola Heiau
44 Puu O'o Ranch

45 St. Benedict's Painted Church (1902)
46 Suisan Dock
47 Thurston Lava Tube
48 Turtle Cave
49 Upolu Airport
50 Volcano House
51 Wahauula Heiau
52 Waikoloa Golf Course
53 Waimea-Kohala Airport
54 Waipio Valley Lookout
55 Wood Valley Camp
56 Kealakekua Bay St. Underw. Park
57 Ahuena Heiau
58 Kona Village Resort, Four Seasons Resort
59 Royal Waikoloan Hotel
60 Mauna Lani Resort
61 Hapuna Beach State Park
62 Parker Ranch Museum
63 Lapakahi State Historical Park
64 Pololu Valley Lookout
65 Wailuku River State Park
66 Lava Tree State Monument
67 Mackenzie State Recreation Area
68 Kumukahi Lighthouse

Land Area:
4.037 square miles
93 miles long
76 miles wide

Population:
Total: 122300
(1989 census estimate)

Highest Elevation:
Mauna Kea 13796 feet (4205 m)

Airports:
Hilo: Hilo International Airport
Kona: Keahole Airport
Kamuela: Waimea-Kohala Airport

Main Seaports:
Hilo Bay
Kawaihae
Kailua-Kona

The original statue of Kamehameha

of sheer ocean cliffs and a black sand beach below. Return towards Hawi but don't blink or you'll miss it on the left: the **Kohala Tong Wo Society building**. Founded in 1886, it's the last of many Chinese societies established on the Big Island. Admire it from the road; it's private property. Look inside **Ackerman Gallery** in Kapa'au before turning south onto Route 250, which climbs Kohala Mountain, residue of an extinct volcano. Follow a high road lined with browsing cattle and windbreaks of eucalyptus, ironwood and Norfolk pines.

Spectacular views – if the vog, or volcanic smog, isn't thick – of Mauna Kea (13,796ft/4205m) and Mauna Loa (13,679ft/4169m) unfold as the road descends through cactus to Waimea.

Waimea is sometimes described as a misty and quaint cow town; it remains misty but with all the new shopping centers, the quaintness somehow fades. (The post office calls the town Kamuela, to distinguish it from Kauai's Waimea. Road signs however say Waimea, as do residents.) It's a company town, sitting on Parker Ranch land, said to be the largest individually-held ranch in America. Just before entering Waimea, stop at **Hale Kea Ranch**, which offers fine lunches and dinners at **Hartwell's**, the restored 1897 ranch manager's residence. In town, the **Edelweiss** and **Merriman's**, both started by culinary escapees from Kohala resorts, are island classics for lunch and dinner.

Should the siren call of beach-time summon, it's but a short drive back to South Kohala and Kona. Otherwise, continue east on Route 19 to Honoka'a and the **Waipi'o Valley Lookout**, 1,000ft (305m) above this huge transcendent valley. Once a powerful social and cultural focal point, it was inhabited by thousands of people for at least a millenium.

The Hale Kea Ranch

Unless you've decided to make a run for Hilo this afternoon, return back through Waimea. I always stop at the **Kamuela Museum**, on the west side of town. It's like a rich and intelligent person's attic put on public display. Vietcong flags share display cases with beautiful antique Chinese ceramics.

Returning to South Kohala, consider a visit to the **Mauna Kea Beach Hotel**, grand-daddy of the Kohala resorts. Its Asian and Pacific art collection is magnificent, as is its small beach. Next door is the newer **Hapuna Beach Prince Hotel**, which sprawls across a bluff above the beach and commands ocean views from here to eternity. Down the coast is the **Mauna Lani Bay Hotel & Bungalows**, which I think is the finest Kohala resort. (Don't be fooled by its lack of theatrics so rampant in newer 'fantasy' resorts. Likewise, don't be fooled by 'bungalows,' if memories of beach bungalows in Thailand or Fiji return; these cost US$2,500 a night.) Explore footpaths around ancient fishponds and shelter caves. Highly recommended are any of its restaurants. Myself, I'd crawl over miles of craggy lava for an outside table at the hotel's **CanoeHouse**, with a plate of lobster won ton ravioli before me and the sunset behind.

Returning towards the highway, follow the signs to the **Puako petroglyph fields**, examples of the fascinating ancient rock drawings which represent scenes of life in pre-contact Hawaii. Further down the coast, another well-marked, 1,000-year-old petroglyph field is at the Waikoloa Resort complex. The **Royal Waikoloan Hotel** has carefully-preserved ancient fishponds.

Late afternoon. Where to settle in for sunset? Anywhere is fine, of course. But **Hapuna Beach**, the island's largest white-sand beach, is perfect.

Or head to **Kailua-Kona**. Known to locals as Kona, the post office as Kailua-Kona, and on maps as Kailua, the leeward side's largest town is the island's social hot spot. Park near the harbor. The King Kamehameha Hotel, on the harbor, offers guided tours of the restored **Ahu'ena Heiau** outside, dedicated to Lono, the fertility deity, and where Kamehameha spent his final days. Walk along Ali'i Drive towards the **Royal Kona Resort**, obvious across the harbor and Kona's best place to stay. Midway is the landmark steeple of **Moku'aikaua Church**, built in 1837 from rock, coral and ohia wood. Finished about the same time is the two-story **Hulihe'e Palace**, once a royal summer retreat.

Sunset is free along the harbor seawall or on the pier. Add dinner to the view at **Jameson's By The Sea** on Ali'i Drive. For fine dining, try the **La Bourgogne** at the Kuakini Plaza, or the more casual **Sibu Cafe** along Ali'i Drive. Better yet, catch a glimpse of Hawaii's most famous chef at **Sam Choy's Restaurant**, a homespun eatery featuring great local food by day and Hawaiian regional cuisine in the evenings.

Petroglyph, Kohala

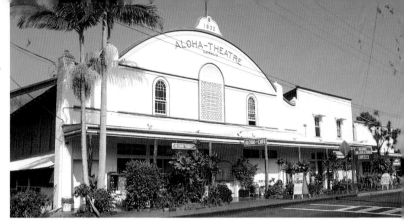

Aloha Theater and Cafe

7. South Kona and South Point

Breakfast in a theater. Lots of chocolate brownies. A powerful, sacred place of refuge. The end of Captain Cook. An old hotel with great pork chops. Coffee beans. America's southernmost point. Thirty-six windmills.

Of course... Do order that freshly-squeezed orange juice, but skip breakfast. A better idea waits elsewhere. Yesterday you went north until there was no more. Today it's south until the same.

From Kona, follow Route 11 towards Honalo, Kainaliu, and Kealakekua, clustered near the bigger town of Captain Cook and nearly impossible for the visitor to tell apart. Note **Teshima's** in Honalo on the left; it's not worth a special drive, but if in the area later and hungry, give it a try for pure local atmosphere. A breakfast worth the drive is waiting for you at the **Aloha Theater Cafe**,

Pu'uhonua o Honaunau

in Kainaliu. Food any time of
the day is good and tempting
(but skip the croissants), especially when eaten on the outside
terrace. Check the community theater schedule then buy a big bag of
their delicious brownies for the road.
Down the road in the town of **Captain Cook** proper is the **Manago Hotel**
on the right, where the menu is simple and
cheap, and known for its lip-smacking pork
chops. The Manago family has owned and operated the hotel for over 70 years. Rooms are basic
but quiet.

Makai of town – towards the ocean – is **Kealakekua
Bay**, a state marine conservation district and the site of
Captain Cook's 1779 dismemberment by insulted and angry
Hawaiians. If time allows later, consider snorkeling here. There's a
heiau and an inaccessible 27-ft (8-m) high white monument on
British territory solemnizing Cook. For now, pass on by.

You're in coffee country, the only place in the United States
where coffee is commercially grown. All along the highway south of
Kona, in the small villages clustered around Captain Cook, Kona
coffee is sold. But there is no urgent need to buy it here, as bean
prices are reasonably consistent from island to island. But it's definitely freshest here. Forget the blends – they're only 10 percent
pure Kona.

Take the turnoff to **Pu'uhonua o Honaunau National Historical
Park**, called the 'city of refuge' by the lazy. Meticulously and accu-

rately restored, it was indeed an ancient
refuge where transgressors and *kapu* vio-
laters were pardoned by priests – but
only after outswimming sharks or scaling
stone walls, and vowing to do penance.
This *pu'uhonua* gained increasing spiritual power, or *mana*, over the centuries as
more and more chiefs were buried here.
When the *kapu* system collapsed in 1819,
so did the *pu'uhonua's* importance. The
guided tours are highly recommended,
and the grounds themselves are wonderful
for idle walking, simple daydreaming, or
inspections of the full-sized primitive
idols and the 1,000-ft (305-m) long, 10-ft
(3-m) high and 17-ft (5½-m) wide **Great
Wall**. Towering coconut palms swing
melodically above.

On the way back to the main road, up
from the historial park, stop at the turn-

St Benedict's Church

of-the-century **St Benedict's Church**, painted inside with biblical scenes and motifs for those unable to read.

Coffee plants and macadamia nut trees give way further south to barren black nothingness – lava flows from 1907, 1919, 1926 and 1950. Inland is the southwest rift zone of Mauna Loa, still active and potent. Forget about the cheap land for sale along the road, and instead take the turnoff for **South Point**. Many guidebooks skip over South Point, pleading a terrible road or empty desolation. Nonsense. The paved road is fine, if not minimal, but watch for oncoming traffic. And the windswept land, like yesterday at Upolu Point, South Point is compelling and powerful.

Half way down, stare at the 36 wind generators spinning like flustered mechanical flowers. Get out and listen to the *whoosh-whoosh-whoosh*. Privately owned, the **Kamoa Wind Farm** produces electricity that's sold to the public utility.

Keep bearing right to the southernmost point in the United States. Sit on the cliff edge near the Kalalea Heiau, where clear blue waters crash against the basalt cliffs. Needless to say, storms are quite impressive here. The first Polynesians to land in Hawaii probably did so here. Fishing is good off the point, attested to by the modern moorings and ladders hanging out over the 50-ft (15-m) high cliffs, and to nearby ancient canoe moorings. Due south is the Antarctic, the nearest landfall.

If the brownies weren't enough, stop in **Na'alehu**, a few more miles east on Route 11. It's a proverbially sleepy town, lovely and lined with monkeypod trees. Try **Na'alehu Coffee Shop** for fresh fish, or the **Na'alehu Fruit Stand**. More upscale is the **Punaluu Black Sands Restaurant**, 10 miles (16km) further in Punalu'u.

If you haven't already, it's time for another decision. About an hour further is **Hawaii Volcanoes National Park** (see *Itinerary 9*). If you got to an early start this morning, it's another three or four hours minimum for an extension to the park. Another possibility for a long day – and I don't recommend this at all – is to completely loop around the island through the park and Hilo, returning to Kohala and Kona from the north. Better is a night in Volcano, if you've planned ahead for reservations, or a night in Hilo, 30 minutes away from each other. Both the park and Hilo deserve more than the quick glance that continuing on now will give you.

Otherwise, backtrack along Route 11 towards Kona, taking your time and maybe exploring some of those side roads that tempted you earlier, like the fishing village of **Miloli'i**, snorkeling and the Captain Cook monument at Kealakekua, or the hillside artist's town of **Holualoa**, above Kailua-Kona. Essential stops in Holualoa: **Kimura Lauhala Shop**, selling things woven from hala leaves; **Kona Art Center**, diverse in range and quality, and years ago the catalyst for Kona's development as a focus for Pacific art; some of the several galleries, especially **Studio 7**. An alternative for lodging in Kona or Kohala is the **Holualoa Inn**, a nice bed-and-breakfast.

If you're staying on in Kona or South Kohala tonight, watch the sunset from wherever impulse takes you. For local eats and atmosphere, try the pork chops at Manago's or dinner at Teshima's (see pages 42/3). For sophisticated dining, change socks and head for the Kohala resorts: **Le Soleil** at the Mauna Lani, **The Grill** or the more formal **Dining Room** at the Ritz-Carlton Mauna Lani, or **The Batik** at the Mauna Kea. After dinner, beautiful little beaches at both hotels and lots of starlight wait patiently outside. Adding to the moon-lit magic of Mauna Kea and Kona Village are streamlined manta rays swimming in and out of the spotlights right offshore.

No refuge

8. Hilo

Hawaii's biggest secret. Volcano lava flows – very fresh, very hot, and very destructive.

Hilo rates high on my list of special places, despite 120ins (305cm) of rain annually. The rain eliminates tourist clutter, but more importantly, it makes Hilo bountiful and rich, and oh-so-tropical. Exploring Hilo and surrounding areas, including Hawaii Volcanoes National Park, is time well spent. If you've added Hilo to Itinerary 6, eliminating Pahoa and Lava Tree State Park frees up time.

Drive to Hilo from the north, along the beautiful Hamakua coast. First impressions of Hilo often underwhelm. Hawaii's second-largest city outside Oahu, Hilo feels more like a big town, which it really is. It certainly harbors no pretenses in humoring the tourist, and thus its charm.

Like Kailua-Kona on the island's opposite side, Hilo's focus is the harbor. Tsunamis – or tidal waves – in 1946 and 1960 destroyed part of the downtown business district, but many of the old buildings remained. Pick up the brochure 'Walking Tour of Historic Downtown.' The intersection of Keawe and Waianuenue is a good reference point; a number of stores and restaurants fill the renovated buildings. Good places to eat: **Bears' Coffee**, a popular hangout noted for its breakfasts; **Roussel's**, serving Cajun-style lunches and dinner; **Lehua's Bar and Restaurant**, with island-type cuisine (meaning creative) and weekend jazz. Down Keawe Street, **Sachi's Gourmet** serves up cheap local Japanese-style meals while Pescatore's has traditional Italian fare.

A few blocks up, the **Lyman Museum and Mission House** is a must visit. This 1839 missionary homestead has impressive 19th-century furniture. Next door, the museum's first floor is dedicated to Hawaiiana. Upstairs is the secret treasure: world-class rock-and-

Kalapana, Pele's intrusions

Kilauea and ocean

mineral and shell collections. In the museum's gift shop, pick up an inexpensive walking tour map of old Hilo.

If you're staying in Hilo, it will be along **Banyan Drive**, Hilo's hotel district. Modest in size and price, the hotels are friendly and accommodating. Best is the **Hawaii Naniloa Hotel**, with excellent views of the bay and Mauna Kea. Opposite is **Lili'uokalani Gardens**, an uncrowded and serene Japanese garden of stone bridges and lions, lanterns, and a tea ceremony pavilion. Just off Banyan Drive on Lihiwai Street is the **Suisan Fish Market**, where early-morning bidding wars in Japanese and heavy pidgin accents are waged between fishermen. The bounty: a colorful display of aku, mahi, ahi and other Hawaiian fish, many of which may show up on tonight's dinner plates.

South of Hilo is a splendid scenic drive down Highway 130 towards the coast and recent lava flows. Stay on Highway 130 until the road is blocked with *pahoehoe* lava. Just beyond, scores of homes were destroyed in recent years, along with the village of **Kalapana**. Towards the ocean, thick steam may billow where molten lava enters the sea. Backtrack to Highway 132, then through a beautiful tunnel of trees towards **Lava Tree State Monument**, where in 1790 molten lava flooded a rainforest, then drained, leaving shells of solidified lava around now-vaporized trees. The common name for this uncommonly beautiful phenomenon is a tree mold: shrouded by mists should you visit in the early morning, the place has an eerie feel. Further on is **Cape Kumukahi**, the island's eastern most point and site of a 1960 lava flow. Route 137 leads westward to **MacKenzie State Recreation Area**, a serene glade of ironwood trees along ocean cliffs. (*As always, lock the car.*)

Cape Kumukahi

Return to **Pahoa**, forgoing the bypass for the main town road lined with raised wooden sidewalks. Once a major supplier of *ohia* wood railroad ties to the mainland, Pahoa has an unusually high concentration of old buildings, a fact that will not be lost on you. Nothing exceptional, but fun.

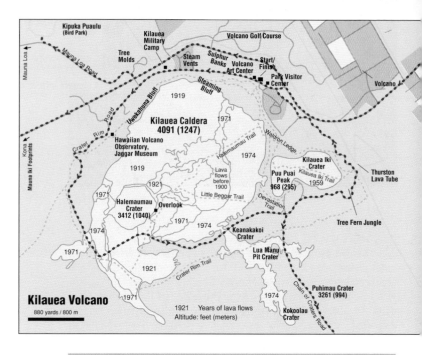

Kilauea Volcano

880 yards / 800 m

1921 Years of lava flows
      Altitude: feet (meters)

Map labels:
Kipuka Puaulu (Bird Park), Kilauea Military Camp, Volcano Golf Course, Mauna Loa, Mauna Loa Road, Tree Molds, Steam Vents, Sulphur Banks, Volcano Art Center, Start/Finish, Park Visitor Center, Volcano, Steaming Bluff, 1919, Uwekahuna Bluff, Kilauea Caldera 4091 (1247), 1971, Waldron Ledge, Crater Rim Road, Kona, Mauna Iki Footprints, Hawaiian Volcano Observatory, Jaggar Museum, 1919, 1974, Halemaumau Trail, Kilauea Iki Crater, Thurston Lava Tube, Lava flows before 1900, Puu Puai Peak 968 (295), Kilauea Iki Trail, 1959, 1921, Little Beggar Trail, Devastation Trail, Halemaumau Crater 3412 (1040), Overlook, 1971, 1974, Tree Fern Jungle, 1971, Keanakakoi Crater, 1974, Lua Manu Pit Crater, 1971, 1921, Crater Rim Trail, Chain of Craters Road, Puhimau Crater 3261 (994), 1974, Kokoolau Crater

9. Hawaii Volcanoes National Park

A red-hot volcano... Cool, misty heights... Art and artists.

Although you can push for half a day, this option really deserves a full day, better yet, three or four. A compromise: stay in Hilo or in Volcano Village, and then fly out from Hilo.

Start at the **Hawaii Volcanoes National Park Visitor Center** for good interpretive exhibits, and for road closure and volcanic activity information. Across the road is Volcano House, a hotel and restaurant perched on the very rim of **Kilauea Caldera**. Unless necessary for convenience, forget sleeping or eating at the hotel. The reputation of this historically-prominent hotel has slipped downhill over the years. Nevertheless, the location is superb, and the hotel's caldera lookout is a must; varying hues of lava on the caldera bottom betray multiple lava flows between 1885 and 1982.

Cross the road to the **Volcano Art Center**, next to the Visitor Center. Volcano is rich in creative talent, and the center's offerings are perhaps unsurpassed anywhere in the islands.

This is the realm of Pele, the volcano goddess. Follow **Crater Rim Drive**. A few minutes past Steaming Bluff, where seeping groundwater hits hot rock, the **Hawaiian Volcano Observatory**, operated by the US Geological Survey, monitors volcanic activity. A must visit is the **Jaggar Museum** next door.

Drive across a 1974 lava flow to the **Halema'uma'u Lookout**. The short path is sometimes veiled in smelly vapors; note the signs and health warnings. Halema'uma'u, a collapsed depression within Kilauea Caldera, is said to be the current abode of Pele. Believers leave gifts of *ti* leaves, coins, and flower leis on the rim.

Turn off onto the **Chain of Craters Road**, a road first opened in 1965 that descends down Mauna Loa's East Rift, which itself descends into the ocean. A new island-to-be, **Loihi**, gestates 3,000ft (915m) below the surface on the east rift and probably 100,000 years from the surface. Once it was possible to loop around to Hilo via this back way through the village of Kalapana, but Pele is often a spunky pest; Kalapana was recently destroyed by lava flows, frequent in this area. When lava flows hit the ocean, spiraling clouds of steam rise furiously hundreds of feet; twilight turns the coast into a surreal red perdition, strangely beautiful.

Returning to the Rim road, drive past the **Kilauea Iki Crater**. In 1959, a 2,000-ft (610-m) high erupting fountain issued skyward from here. The **Devastation Trail** is a somber meditation, countered by a rain forest walk to, and through, the **Thurston Lava Tube**. Other surprises demand your time: **Pua'ulu** (Bird Park); the **Tree Molds**; and my favorite, the **Mauna Iki Footprints**. As Kamehameha I was consolidating his rule over the Big Island, some fleeing warriors died on the Ka'u Desert from Kilauea's toxic gases and ash. Their footprints solidified in the ash. It's an easy trail, one of many that slice throughout the park.

Volcano Village is just minutes from the park entrance. A lot of artists have gravitated, if you can say that, to this 3,700-ft elevation (1,128-m) community. It's a quiet, reflective place. Rather than staying at the Volcano House, or even eating there, try the **Kilauea Lodge**, reservations recommended, or else the **Volcano Country Club** restaurant. (Yes, there's a golf course up here.) Several bed and breakfast options are also in the area.

A new beach in the making

Kauai

Until a few years ago, there was no stop light anywhere on Kauai. Things have changed, quickly and irreversibly: roads are being widened, shopping centers shoot up, and traffic chokes up at times. But of all the four main islands, Kauai remains the most rural, the most wild, and perhaps the most enchanting. It's a stubborn island, both in its geographical inaccessibility and in the character of its people, as Kamehameha I learned when he tried unsuccessfully to conquer Kauai.

Testimony to the spirit and strength of Kauai is the speed with which the island bounced back after the onslaught of Hurricane Iniki in 1992. Most attactions and businesses were up and running after two years and Mother nature has quickly healed the landscape to perfection.The oldest of the inhabited islands, Kauai is probably the closest to what a tropical fantasy island *should* look like: steep

North Shore, Hanalei Bay in distance

11

green cliffs and mountainsides bedecked with cascading waterfalls seeming to fall forever; rumors of lost valleys and secretive small people called the Menehune and Mu; beaches so inaccessible and so perfect that an advertising art director couldn't do better.

Our first two full-day itineraries split the island in half, pivoting on the most southern point where many of the resorts and most of the sunshine is: Poipu. Lihue, the commercial and governmental hub, is half an hour west, but with limited accommodations. Further along the eastern coast, there are a few moderately-priced hotels and resorts.

A North Shore sunset from the Princeville Hotel

Itinerary 10 takes you along and above Kauai's dry leeward coast, high up to the edge of Kauai's interior and an unexpected chasm in the island. *Itinerary 11* swings the other way, along the wet east coast to the north shore. Give serious thought to a night or two on the North Shore.

Itineraries 12 and *13* focus on the urban: the contemporary center of Lihue and the ancient center of Wailua. These are short options, close to the resorts and easily done in half a day, or combined into a day. Also possible is adding the Lihue option to the end of *Itinerary 10*, and Wailua either to the start or end of *Itinerary 11*.

10. Waimea Canyon and the Leeward Coast

A breakfast sampling of fattening pastries in old sugar towns, a Russian fortress, Captain Cook's first landfall in Hawaii, the heights – and depths – of Waimea Canyon and Koke'e. End with an elegant dinner to make up for the breakfast nibbling.

When the birds start twittering outside, hit the road early, not because there's a lot of driving ahead, but because you're selfish. You'd rather not share Waimea Canyon with bus loads of tourists.

51

Skip a hotel breakfast, unless linen napkins and polished silver are vital. A number of places enroute encourage exploratory nibbling. *You're going up high, so bring a warm jacket or sweater.*

Koloa, a few minutes up the road from Poipu, is a compact place, once a sugar town but now crammed with boutiques, restaurants and souvenir stores. Everything will be closed right now except **Lappert's**, serving up pastries, muffins and coffee. But remember, there's more up the road. From Koloa, Route 53 leads to the main island highway, Route 50. If staying in Lihue or beyond, join the itinerary here. As the road descends westward, rolling sugar cane fields climb right up to the foothills on your right. There's probably a brooding veil of clouds higher up at 5,147ft (1,600m), where the map says **Mt Wai'ale' ale** should be. I've never ever seen this remnant of Kauai's single volcano – from either the ground or the air. That it gets a *minimum* of 450ins (1,143cm) of rain annually could explain its fleetingness. But no worries. Hawaiian weather can be extremely local; just 20 miles (32km) from Wai'ale'ale – the world's rainiest place – it hardly rains at all.

Drive past Ele'ele and Port Allen. A couple of blinks beyond, watch for **Hanapepe** and head into town. Like most sugar towns now, Hanapepe looks passed up by the future. But there's a renewed spark simmering in town. The road passes

Kauai

5 miles / 8 km

Altitude: feet (meters)

Itinerary 10
Itinerary 11
Itinerary 12
Itinerary 13

Pacif

Puanaiea P

Makaha Point

MILOLI

POLIHALE STATE PARK

Makole
Polihale
27
12

BARKING SANDS BEACH
Nohili Point

W A I N

Mana

Mana Point
50

Kaulakahi

Kokole Point

Kekaha
Oomano Point
Kikuc

Channel

WRIGHT BEACH F

Mana Road

5

Points of Interest

1 Alakai Swamp
2 Dry Cave (Haena)
3 Fern Grotto (Near Wailua)
4 Fishing Shrines (South Coast)
5 Hanalei Plantation Museum
6 Hauola o Honaunau (Wailua)
7 Hikina o Kala Heiau (Wailua)
8 Ho'ai Heiau (Near Kukui'ula)
9 Holoholoku Heiau (Wailua)
10 Kalalau Valley Lookout
11 Kaneiolouma Heiau
12 Kapaula Heiau (Barking Sands Beach)
13 Kapinao Heiau
14 Hanalei Lookout
15 Kipapa Heiau (Kilauea Bay)
16 Koke'e Lodge and Museum
17 Kukui o Lono Golf Course
18 Last Eruption on Kauai
19 Lohiau's Hula Platform
20 Lihue Airport
21 Malae Heiau & Petroglyphs
22 Menehune Ditch (About a m
   stream-mauka on the Waime
23 Menehune Fishpond (Alakok
24 Olu Pua Botanical Gardens

a string of art galleries in old storefronts, worth a look on the return. For now, continue breakfast: pastries, espresso and smoothies at **Hanapepe Bookstore & Espresso** in town, or a Kauai-style omelet with Portuguese sausage at the **Green Garden Restaurant**, near the highway.

Outside Hanapepe, down by the ocean, are ancient salt ponds, but there's not much to see. Continue to Waimea. Just before town,

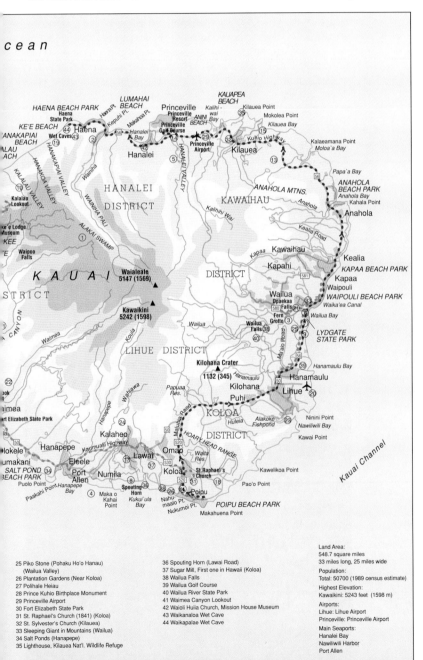

Land Area:
548.7 square miles
33 miles long, 25 miles wide

Population:
Total: 50700 (1989 census estimate)

Highest Elevation:
Kawaikini: 5243 feet (1598 m)

Airports:
Lihue: Lihue Airport
Princeville: Princeville Airport

Main Seaports:
Hanalei Bay
Nawiliwili Harbor
Port Allen

25 Piko Stone (Pohaku Ho'o Hanau)
    (Wailua Valley)
26 Plantation Gardens (Near Koloa)
27 Polihale Heiau
28 Prince Kuhio Birthplace Monument
29 Princeville Airport
30 Fort Elizabeth State Park
31 St. Raphael's Church (1841) (Koloa)
32 St. Sylvester's Church (Kilauea)
33 Sleeping Giant in Mountains (Wailua)
34 Salt Ponds (Hanapepe)
35 Lighthouse, Kilauea Nat'l. Wildlife Refuge

36 Spouting Horn (Lawai Road)
37 Sugar Mill, First one in Hawaii (Koloa)
38 Wailua Falls
39 Wailua Golf Course
40 Wailua River State Park
41 Waimea Canyon Lookout
42 Waioli Huiia Church, Mission House Museum
43 Waikanaloa Wet Cave
44 Waikapalae Wet Cave

A Russian fort

the ruins of **Fort Elizabeth** recall a strange, fascinating, and mostly insignificant episode in Hawaii's history. In 1815, a Russian ship was shipwrecked near Waimea, and Kauai's king claimed its cargo. An agent of the czar was sent to negotiate return of the valuable cargo. He got carried away and tried to negotiate for a slice of Hawaii as well. The fort was begun in 1816 as part of the deal, but the deal collapsed – the czar preferred Alaska instead. Climb the fort's red rock walls to take in Waimea Bay, where Captain Cook made his first Hawaiian landfall; in downtown Waimea is an undistinguished monument – an understatement almost – to his 1778 arrival.

Waimea Canyon

In **Waimea**, turn inland for Waimea Canyon Road. But first, stop at **Yumi's**. The window says, 'sushi and pies', but inside heavenly cinnamon rolls await. Now, onward. Waimea Canyon Road weaves and lumbers upward, eventually yielding to rousing views of Waimea Canyon. There are several lookouts where you can watch mists, rainbows, shadows and colors shift like atmospheric alchemy in this 3,500-ft (1,060-m) deep, 10-mile (16-km) long chasm.

Further is a fork in the road: left to **Kalalau Valley Lookout**, right to **Koke'e State Park**. Go left. Kalalau Valley is postcard-perfect and nothing less. But the view of Kalalau is quite temperamental and whimsical; it may be there or not, obscured by clouds and mists below. If so, wait a few minutes or return later, or at last resort, buy a postcard. If not visible, here's what you're missing: the swooping valley drops 4,000ft (1,200m) down to a beautiful beach, the terminus of an 11-mile (17-km) hiking trail originating at the other end of the Na Pali Coast, near Hanalei. The valley is ennobled by steep, graceful, and vibrantly-green cliff walls.

Swing back to Koke'e State Park, an important refuge for many of Hawaii's indigenous – and endangered – birds. **Koke'e Lodge** has a dozen economical and rustic cabins, and a decent finish to your breakfast survey, if still hungry, is at the restaurant nearby. Nothing elegant, but satisfying in this high, cool air. Stop at the museum for a brief on the area's natural history, and for walking and hiking information.

For Mom . . .

COCONUT POSTCARDS IS FUN FUN

Follow the road back down to the coast, keeping right at the fork midway. At the bottom drive through the tidy neighborhoods of **Kekaha**, past the hissing sugar mill and onto Route 50. You could backtrack towards Waimea, but why not continue to road's end? Why not, indeed, for **Polihale State Park** will surprise you with a big and moody beach and even bigger and moodier cliffs. Follow the signs. Forget about swimming at Polihale, but do contemplate the waves, and the cliffs to the north, the start of the awesome Na Pali Coast. Nearby are the ruins of the **Polihale Heiau**, difficult to find. This is a sacred place where spirits of the dead leap into the afterlife.

Return to Waimea past sunny, scenic, and almost always nearly-empty beaches. Tempted? Plenty of time. Curious about that flat-top island across the way? It's **Niihau**, inhabited, Hawaiian-speaking, and no tourists allowed, thank you. Hungry? In Waimea, stop at the **International Museum & Cafe** on Route 50, a big airy place with friendly people and fine food. The walls are filled with exotic and unusual artifacts from Asia, many from Tibet. It's all for sale.

The 1856 St Raphael's Chruch

If early morning views up topside were hidden, consider a return to Waimea and Koke'e.

South on Route 50, watch for **Olokele** on the right. A one-company town, its main street is lined with timeworn monkeypod trees and classic old street lamps. At the end of the road is the Olokele Sugar Co office and mill. Stop again in Hanapepe to visit the stores and art galleries. Lunch possibilities include this morning's breakfast places, but check for any tour buses first. Send a coconut postcard from **Kauai Fine Arts Gallery**.

Stay on Route 50 to Route 530, which funnels you back to Koloa via an impressive tunnel of eucalyptus trees, planted in 1911. Or consider continuing to Lihue (see *Itinerary 12*).

In Koloa, scout the shops along old wooden sidewalks. Across from the main shopping area is a stone chimney, what's left of Kauai's first sugar mill built in 1835. Drive a couple miles to **St Raphael's Church**, built in 1856 and a pleasant place to rest. Signs guide the way. A mile east is a small hill called Pu'uhi, which let loose Kauai's last volcanic eruption.

If it's approaching sunset, time to sit. The Poipu beach area is perfect, either from the sand or at **Brennecke's Beach Broiler** along Hoone Road. For an elegant evening, try dinner at **Roy's Poipu Bar & Grill** in the Poipu Shopping Village, or **Tidepools** at the Hyatt Regency Kauai. A short drive away in Puhi is **Gaylord's**, outdoors at a 1930s estate. For any of these last three restaurants, put on a pair of shoes. Flip-flops won't cut it. Nightlife is limited on Kauai, and rightfully so. Dancers head for **Kuhio's** disco at the Hyatt or **Legends Nightclub** in Nawiliwili. The Hyatt has a wood-paneled bar called **Stevenson's Library**, good for a sophisticated game of pool. More appropriate are the Hawaiian songs performed weekends at the **Grove Restaurant** at Waimea Plantation Cottages.

11. Hanalei and the North Shore

Maybe the most beautiful place on earth. Along the way: ancient sites, a lighthouse and birds with 8-ft (2½-m) wingspans, a prince of a golf resort, an old bridge with omnipotent powers.

Today you can't get on the road early enough, not to outrun tour buses like yesterday, but simply because one of the most stunning places anywhere waits patiently on the North Shore: Hanalei and road's end. If possible, consider a night – or a hundred – conceding the siren power of Hanalei. Take an umbrella.

From Poipu, find Highway 50 and drive east towards Lihue. Depending on the time, a morning rush hour of sorts may be going into Lihue; although perhaps a surprise, it doesn't last long or far. Continue through Lihue and on to Wailua, both covered in Itineraries 12 and 13. It's possible to do part or all of the Wailua portion here, for example, **Poli'ahu Heiau** and **Opaeka'a Falls**.

A few minutes beyond Wailua is **Kapa'a**, a humming and popping town with no touristy sights except restaurants and stores. Stop by **Michelle's Cafe & Bakery** for breakfast and pastries. For something heftier and traditional, the **Ono Family Restaurant** is popular. In the Hee Fat Marketplace, note **Jimmy's Grill** for a later lunch. (Don't be discouraged by the sand on the ground floor.) Recommended for dinner on the return is the Hawaiian regional cuisine at **A Pacific Cafe**.

The road eases around the northeast edge of Kauai to the north shore. A must visit: **Kilauea National Wildlife Refuge**, not for the 1913 lighthouse – said to have the world's largest (12-ft/3½-m high) clamshell lens – but rather for the gorgeous views of the coast and wondrous seabirds riding the wind. Watch out especially for the frigate bird, hard to ignore with its 8-ft (2½-m) wingspan. Odds are uncertain, but scan the ocean 700ft (210m) below for turtles, whales, dolphins, and the rare Hawaiian monk seal. Bad eyes? Borrow a pair of binoculars at the visitors center.

Kilauea Point

Coming or going to the lighthouse, stop in Kilauea town at the **Kong Lung Store**, an 1881 plantation general store. Even the crankiest of shoppers can find something here. A tomato's throw away is **Casa di Amici**, with relaxing ambiance and excellent pasta – and a good wine list, too. Lighter fare is at **Banana Joe's** fruit stand, back on the main highway.

The highway sifts through gentle open countryside towards the Princeville Airport, with scheduled flights by prop plane to Honolulu. **Papillon Helicopters** has its base here for tours to Na Pali and Waimea. The road starts to narrow, anticipating an even narrower road later on.

You can't miss it: the 1,000-acre (400-ha) **Princeville Resort**, named after Kamehameha IV's son, Prince Albert. Blessed with exceptional scenery, even by Hawaii standards, the resort has two world-class golf courses, a large clubhouse, a shopping centre and

Princeville Resort and Hanalei Bay

Sit down here

luxurious houses and condos. Drive through the resort to the **Princeville Hotel**, recently renovated into one of Hawaii's nicest luxury hotels. (I think the staff here is one of Hawaii's best.) Walk through the airy lobby, done in an elegant Mediterranean motif, but eventually the view outside yanks you to the immense windows overlooking **Hanalei Bay** and **Mount Makana** beyond (erroneously called Bali Hai, from the movie *South Pacific*, filmed in Hanalei). Hanalei Bay is a favorite spot of yachtsmen in summer, giving way to surfers in winter when the big waves from the north roll in. The Princeville's **Cafe Hanalei** serves up both the view and excellent meals. If you are in Hanalei tonight, reserve a window table – open to the breeze and stars and the expansive bay – at **La Cascata** Italian restaurant.

On the main highway beyond the Princeville entrance is a lookout of **Hanalei Valley**, which provides half of Hawaii's poi from the cultivated taro fields below. More importantly, the wetlands offer refuge for birds; the lower extent of Hanalei Valley is a national wildlife refuge. (That tall and lanky white bird seemingly everywhere is the cattle egret.)

The road twists down to the Hanalei River. A 1913 vintage one-lane bridge, cherished by local residents because it effectively bans tour buses from continuing any further, carries you across.

Hanalei is home to an interesting community, a life-style stew of true *kama'aina*, surfers, New Age types, bankers and celebrities in hiding, a couple of astronauts, and more than its far share of beach bums. The main commercial center is **Ching Young Village**, good for bee pollen, *The New York Times*, T-shirts or camping gear. The **Shell House** is swell for its eclectic menu and laid-back attitudes; close by is **Tahiti Nui**, famous throughout the Pacific as a properly funky and friendly place to drink a cold beer, and for a properly-fun luau on Wednesday and Friday nights.

Down the road on the left is a New England-looking green church. This is the **Wai'oli Hui'ia Church**, more easily pronounced 'the green church.' Visit the **Wai'oli Mission House Museum** just behind the church.

The road from Hanalei to the end of civilization is distinctly rural as it winds through picturesque streams and one-lane bridges (observe the first-come, first-cross etiquette), passing beautiful empty beaches and simple houses on million-dollar plots of land. At the far end of Hanalei Bay, directly opposite the

Cattle egret

Princeville Hotel, the road begins to twist and shoot past **Luma-ha'i Beach**, made famous in *South Pacific*. A truly a beautiful beach, it is flanked by black lava rock. Despite its fame and day-time popularity, I've experienced dozens of dusks from the beach alone, with not another soul in sight.

The **Hanalei Colony Resort** further along has condo-style accommodations, simple in personality but almost directly on the beach. A family with children couldn't do better. **Charo's**, on the main road leading north is equally accommodating for eats, with a *cuchi-cuchi* view of the Pacific literally just outside.

Around **Ha'ena Beach** are several caves along the road. Called **wet or dry** caves for obvious reasons, they are actually ancient lava tubes, some extending a mile back. Another couple of minutes further is the end of the road and **Ke'e Beach**. Midday is crowded here, as are weekends. In summer, the snorkeling's quite good, but winter turns the waves into monsters. Better to sit and watch. The trailhead for the Kalalau Trail (Remember yesterday's lookout?) starts here: Eleven miles (18km) of gorgeous but strenuous trail snake along the Na Pali coastline, skirting isolated beaches and ocean caves. The first two miles (one mile up, one mile down) lead to pristine Hanakapiai Beach, a favorite destination for a half-day hike with picnic. *Do not swim at Hanakapiai. The currents are dangerous here.* If a serious hike is out of the question, opt for a motorized raft trip along the coast – highly recommended – with **Captain Zodiac** (see the *Activities* chapter). Near the trailhead is the **Lohiau's Hula Platform**, dedicated to the goddess of hula.

Despite lots of people during the day, sunsets usually blossom on a nearly-empty Ke'e Beach, a persuasive argument in my book for staying late or all night in Hanalei.

A wet cave along Ha'ena Beach

An easy couple of hours: a 1930s estate converted into shops and a restaurant, Menehune handiwork, a look at modern resort handiwork, and, yes, a museum. Noodles, too.

Kauai's recent history is virtually synonymous with the Wilcox name, one of the early missionary families. **Kilohana**, on Route 50 between Poipu and Lihue, is one of the Wilcoxes' seemingly-countless grand old estates. The rooms of this 1930s 16,000-sq ft (1,400-sq m) Tudor-style mansion are filled by boutiques, with some of the island's finest shopping. Around a courtyard outside is one of the island's best restaurants, **Gaylord's**.

Like nearly every other town on Kauai, Lihue started with sugar. It's now Kauai's largest community and its governmental seat. It's not a tourist locus, but there are a couple of things to see. Begin at the **Kauai Museum**, on Rice Street. Once the public library, the museum packs a lot of natural history and people history into an hour or two. Open on weekdays and Saturday mornings, the museum often offers half-day courses in *lauhala* weaving and lei-making If there's any essential shopping or banking to be done, the museum is surrounded by both. Buy a pint of milk; don't ask questions, you'll find out why.

Continue down Rice Street towards Nawiliwili, Kauai's picturesque but commercial harbor. At the pier where the inter-island cruise ships dock, bear right past a huge, monolithic gray warehouse – stored sugar cane for shipment to the mainland – to Hulemalu Road. The road climbs to a lookout on the left. Feed the black cat with the milk; you may have to call it. Below you is the **Alakoko Fishpond**, fed by the

Gaylord's at Kilohana

Hule'ia Stream descending from the Hoary Head Mountains beyond. Sometimes called the **Menehune Fishpond**, legend says the Menehune – little leprechaun-like people gifted with amazing building skills and here long before the Polynesians arrived – built the pond. An ancient example of aqua-farming, this pond is part of the **Huleia National Wildlife Refuge**, home to several endangered waterfowl species.

Return to Nawiliwili and head for the Kauai Lagoons resort, home of the Kauai Marriott. Formerly called the Westin Kauai, it was a Hawaii fantasy resort, one of those places people love or people hate, nothing in between. Now, although it has reopened as the Marriott, there are remnants of the old Westin, like huge marble columns and an opulent octagonal swimming pool. Other elements

Menehune Fishpond

of the property have been reworked to fit more into the Kauai setting. For instance, where once there were galloping marble horses spouting water in the courtyard, now there is a lush tropical garden with pools, benches and torchlit paths. Whatever you think about the hotel, consider some fresh seafood at **Duke's Canoe Club**, one of Kauai's favorite hangouts, with surfing memorabilia and nice ocean views. A cheaper alternative is back in town, at **Hamura Saimin**, on Kress Street, serving the islands' finest noodle soup, Hawaiian-style.

13. Wailua

Investigations of the royal places along the Wailua River.

Highway 56 leads from Lihue towards **Wailua**, about 10 miles (16km) up the road. Around where the **Wailua River** meets the ocean are a large number of ancient Hawaiian sites. The royal Hawaiians held this area as sacred, and thus *kapu* to commoners. You could poke around for hours, preferably in the early morning or late afternoon. Before crossing the Wailua River bridge, turn right for **Lydgate State Park**, a favorite local beach with full facilities and a nice, protected swimming area. Walk towards the river. A grove of coconut palms shelters the **Hauola o Honaunau**, a place of refuge for fugitives in old Hawaii, and the **Hikina o Kala Heiau**. As with all Hawaiian sites, take care as these places remain sacred for many Hawaiians.

Just after the bridge, turn left onto Highway 580. Two miles (3km) up on the right is a parking lot for **Opaeka'a Falls**, most spectacular after heavy rains on Mt Wai'ale'ale. You can't see them, but shrimp lay eggs in the pool at the bottom of the 40-ft (12-m) waterfall. Walk across the road for a broad view of the Wailua

River gently snaking below, once lined with secret sacred temples all the way up to its origin on Wai'ale'ale; cliffs and bluffs along the way were *ali'i* burial places.

On the river, barge-like boats carry paying tourists to **Fern Grotto**, where ferns grow profusely at the mouth of a lava tube. It's commercially promoted ad nauseam as a must-see but is actually quite ignorable (and I recommend doing just that) because of the intrusive showbiz style of the tour operator, both on the river and at the grotto. Better to spend your time and money renting a kayak and paddling up the river at your own pace, poking along past ancient homesites and thick tropical foliage. No forced serenades, no elbow-to-elbow crowds, just the beauty that is Kauai. Bring a picnic, take your time.

Pay attention

NOTICE —
THIS SITE IS SACRED TO
THE HAWAIIAN PEOPLE
PLEASE SHOW RESPECT

THE WALLS ARE DANGEROUSLY UNSTABLE
PLEASE DO NOT MOVE ROCKS
OR CLIMB ON WALLS *Mahalo Nui*

Back on Highway 580, close to the main highway, there are several sacred outdoor shrines, including the **Poli'ahu Heiau**. Nearby is a bell stone, which rang out when hit with a stone to announce royal births. **Holoholoku Heiau**, a sacrificial altar with royal birthstones nearby, is an older heiau, and has more than coincidental resemblance to Tahitian temples. The rest of the day, get into the local pace of life. If you want to pick up some postcards, bypass the sprawling tourist-oriented Coconut Marketplace, where the prices are high and the souvenirs verge on the tacky. Instead, drop by the local supermarket or drugstore. Take in one of the weekly county-sponsored **Sunshine Markets**, where the fresh produce and flowers are in abundance.

Grab some homemade Portuguese bean soup and homemade pie at **Ono Family Restaurant** on Highway 56. If evening approaches, catch sunset from the beach. For dinner, head back to **A Pacific Cafe** in Kapa'a or stop at **Gaylord's** on the way back to Poipu. If you're ready for some laughs, check out the weekly **Comedy Club** at the Outrigger Kauai Beach Hotel and Villas, close to Lihue.

Romp on Wailua River

Maui

Nobody traveling to Hawaii ever says they're going to Oahu, the Big Island, or Kauai. But they can say *I'm going to Maui*. Indeed, Maui's recognition quotient – not to mention its array of shopping and cuisine – is exceeded in Hawaii only by Oahu's Waikiki.

Maui is just the tip of a tropical iceberg, so to speak. Hawaii's second largest island and the only island namesake of a god, Maui is the exposed top of a 30,000-ft (9,144-m) high mountain. Two volcanoes formed Maui: the older and eroded West Maui volcano, and Haleakala, topping out at 10,023ft (3,055m). The largest dormant volcano on earth, Haleakala necessarily defines Maui's size and character. Its rainshadow yields two superb and sunny beach areas, Ka'anapali in West Maui, and Wailea/Kihei in South Maui. Haleakala's gentle slopes nurture a winery, world-class artists, some of the best onions anywhere, some weird but fascinating flowers, and one of the few remaining preserves of indigenous Hawaiian flora and fauna.

The full-day tours (see *Itinerary 14* and *15*) favor time flexibility. If you're demonically possessed, a few hours will do. If slothfully disposed, the itineraries can last from dawn to dusk, and then some more. *Itinerary 14* hugs the West Maui Mountains, with Lahaina or Ka'anapali as start and finish. It's a good day for roaming, browsing and shopping. A prodigious number of restaurants baits us relentlessly. *Itinerary 15* has loftier ambitions: nothing short of the very summit of Haleakala. Later, you'll wander across Haleakala's lower slopes, known as Upcountry.

The Hana Highway, and Molokai and Lanai (see *Itineraries 16* and *17*) are full-day tours at minimum, but highly recommended nonetheless. The first is a meandering drive to the very eastern edge of the island, where one of the island's most bucolic towns awaits: Hana. *Itinerary 17* includes the islands of Molokai and Lanai, although certainly less cosmopolitan than Maui, but equally fascinating. Each island is worthy of day trips from Maui. Better yet, budget more time so that you can spend a night or two on each one.

Maui

Highest Elevation:
Red Hill (above Haleakala
Crater: 10023 feet (3055 m)

Airports:
Hana: Hana Airport
Kahului: Kahului Airport
Kaanapali: West Maui Airport

Main Seaports:
Lahaina
Kahului Bay
Napili Bay
Hana Bay

Land Area:
728.2 square miles
48 miles long,
26 miles wide

Population:
Total 97100
(1989 census estimate)

49 Satelite Tracking Station, Univ. of Hawaii Lunar and Solar Observatory
50 Waimoku Falls Trail
51 Thompson Stables
52 Waianapanapa State Park
53 Wananalua Church (1838)
54 Maui Tropical Plantation
55 Iao Valley State Park
56 Whalers Village Museum
57 Park Headquarters
58 Kula Botanical Gardens
59 Ihiho o Iehowa o na Kaua Church (1860)
60 Baldwin House
61 Wo Hing Temple
62 Lahaina Jodo Mission

Trails (Haleakala):
Halemau'u Trail
Kaupo Trail (private)
Sliding Sands Trail

- - - - Itinerary 14
.... Itinerary 15
.... Itinerary 16

Altitude: feet (meters)

10 miles / 16 km

Pacific Ocean

WEST MAUI

An easy day in West Maui: Iao Valley State Park, Wailuku, hotels and shopping and eating in Ka'anapali and Kapalua. Maybe a side trip to South Maui. Sunset and dinner in Lahaina.

Sleep late, get up early – it doesn't matter, for today's itinerary is relaxed. Your day centers around West Maui, starting and finishing in Lahaina or Ka'anapali. If staying in South Maui, you'll intercept the itinerary between Lahaina and Wailuku.

You can't help but notice the **West Maui Mountains**, an eroded and extinct volcano, now lusciously green and often embroidered with rainbows. A valley – once the volcano's crater – is your first stop. Only Route 30 heads south out of Lahaina: take it, passing beach parks with clear views across the Au'au Channel of **Molokai**, **Lanai**, and **Kahoolawe**, all part of Maui County. Between November and April, humpback whales nurture newborn-young in the sheltered waters. In season, stop and watch.

The road bends inland across lowlands connecting West Maui with **Haleakala**, the conspicuous and dormant volcano to the right. Signs point to Wailuku, Maui's government seat and an old sugar town nestled in the foothills above the more commercial Kahului. Continue on through both Kahului and Wailuku; you'll stop in Wailuku later.

Iao Valley State Park – the volcano's ancient crater at road's

end – is idyllic, verdantly green, and indubitably wet – 408ins (1,036cm) of rain falls yearly on the 5,788-ft (1,764-m) high Pu'u Kukui nearby; Lahaina, just 8 miles (13km) away by air, gets 20ins (50cm). A stream skirts **Iao Needle**, the valley's 1,200-ft (366-m) high focus, then descends to Wailuku, which means 'water of destruction' – a bloody battle was fought here during Kamehameha's 1790 Maui conquest.

Returning to **Wailuku**, turn left onto Market Street, then to Vineyard Street. This business neighborhood is undergoing modest renovation and is good for a reconnoiter. Several so-called antique shops are clustered here, filled mostly with dusty but wonderful old things and some tantalizing Hawaiiana memorabilia. Wailuku also

Iao Valley

has some interesting crafts shops. Stop by the **Maui Rehabilitation Center** on Mahalani Street, which has good prices on locally-made works. Two casual but quality Thai restaurants – **Siam Thai** on Market and **Saeng's Thai Cuisine** on Vineyard – lure travelers and locals alike for lunch or dinner. For local atmosphere, **Sam Sato's**, further along down Market Street, is perfect for noodles and manju. Have a hankering for a museum? **Hale Ho'ike'ike** – the Bailey Missionary House – is a good museum of both traditional Hawaiian and missionary life.

Leaving Wailuku, dash through Kahului, which has little of interest except essential shopping. But do consider a side trip to **South Maui**, especially Wailea and Makena, with beaches and sunshine as good as, if not better,

A signature Botero sculpture

than Ka'anapali. Bypass Kihei, a nihilistic strip of condos and shopping centers. **Wailea**, in counterpoint, is a well-planned luxury resort with several hotels. Two of the older hotels – **Renaissance**

Wailea Beach Resort and the **Maui Inter-Continental** – seem to get better with age, without the fantasy embellishments of some newer Hawaii hotels. For a bit of sly and fun humor, take a look at the **Fernando Botero sculptures** at the **Grand Wailea Resort, Hotel & Spa**.

Follow Routes 31 and 30 back to West Maui. Save Lahaina for last, so you'll bypass both it and Ka'anapali on your way north to **Kapalua Bay Hotel & Villas**, a low-profile but extremely choice resort. Besides superb golf and accommodation, the food (try **The Grill & Bar** for lunch, and **The Bay Club** for dinner; jacket required) and shopping are among Maui's choicest.

Return towards Ka'anapali, or continue to **Honokohau** (not to be confused with Honokahua, which is closer to Ka'anapali), a small village on

Ka'anapali surfing dude

the coast amidst rugged views and pristine quiet.

Ka'anapali was developed as Hawaii's first planned resort over

30 years ago. Seven luxury hotels pepper Ka'anapali's three miles of white sand and consistent sun. A walkway along the beach offers fun people-watching and hotel reconnaissance. As Hawaii's first so-called fantasy resort, the **Hyatt Regency Maui** is often the *de facto* resort reference for comparisons of Ka'anapali hotels, if not all of Hawaii. The **Westin Maui** seduces many with waterfalls, swimming lagoons, and the sheer ambition of its elegance. Less elaborate is the **Maui Marriott**, comfortably nestled in the shadow of flashier neighbors – and a very comfortable place to stay. **Whalers Village**, wedged amidst the hotels, is a center filled with shops and restaurants. Don't miss the 40-ft (12-m) long sperm whale skeleton outside and an excellent whaling museum upstairs.

Speaking of whaling... South of Ka'anapali, take the first turnoff for **Lahaina**, the Pacific's whaling capital in the early 1800s. It's hard to get lost in Lahaina. Its main street is **Front Street**, paralleling the waterfront. The green-and-white **Pioneer Inn** and nearby banyan tree are good navigation references. The banyan tree is *the* **Banyan Tree**, planted in 1873 by the town sheriff and now extending its canopy nearly an acre. Until the late 1950s, the Pioneer Inn, built in 1901 for inter-island ferry passengers, was the only West Maui hotel. Its not-so-quiet rooms are plain and economical. Behind is a harbor filled with charter boats. The square-rigger *Carthaginian II* is hard to miss.

Don't ignore Lahaina's side streets. Take a look at two cozy and

Fossilized salt

elegant hotels down Lahainaluna Road. The **Lahaina Hotel**, recently renovated and packed with collectible antiques, has waterfront views. Further down is the **Plantation Inn**, with a swimming pool. Both are delightful resort alternatives, each with a fine restaurant.

Available most everywhere is a brochure outlining a historical walking tour. Two suggested stops are the **Wo Hing Temple**, built by a Chinese fraternal society in 1912 and now showing old Thomas Edison films of Hawaii, and the **Baldwin House**, across from the Pioneer Inn. At the top end of Front Street is the **Lahaina Jodo Mission**, where the largest Buddha outside of Asia ponders sunsets and yet more sunsets.

Plantation Inn

In Lahaina, what's new is in equal abundance to what's old. One of the internationally known **Planet Hollywood** restaurants presides on Front Street, with its bizarre assortment of movie memorabilia. The **Hard Rock Cafe** is equally popular with the young and energetic. And don't let Lahaina's size fool you; they've crammed so many boutiques and art galleries along its narrow streets that you can shop till you drop. Lahaina is perfect for spontaneous tramping, but if sunset approaches, drop anchor. Lahaina is also one of the few places in Hawaii with several pubs and restaurants right on the water – **Kimo's** for seafood; **Cheeseburger in Paradise** for the obvious and for lively music; **Lahaina Fish Co** because they catch their own fish in their own boat. In fact, eating in Lahaina is a befuddling problem of decision: **Avalon**, **Longhi's**, **Alex's Hole in the Wall**, **Gerard's**, **David Paul's Lahaina Grill**... The list could continue.

Lahaina stays open late by Hawaii standards, and the night is limited only by your stamina, money, and tomorrow's schedule, which *might include a predawn wake up call*. It's your vacation, after all.

Lahaina's Front Street

The top of Haleakala. (Don't forget warm clothes.) A winery and strange flowers. Windsurfers and cowboys.

It's to be a wondrous day atop **Haleakala**, a dormant – meaning definitely not extinct – volcano. Haleakala roughly translates as 'house used by the sun,' appropriate for the summit sunrises and sunsets. Depending on what you did or didn't do last night, you might consider watching the Pacific's finest sunrise from atop Haleakala (10,023ft/3,040m). Note the qualifier, *might*. A summit sunrise requires a three-in-the-morning wake-up call. If you pass on sunrise, you'll need an early start anyway – by seven at the latest – as the summit often vanishes beneath clouds by late morning. Bring warm clothes; there's a 30-degree difference between the beach and Haleakala's summit, usually amplified by a wind chill factor.

Start near Kahului airport on Route 36. There's a turnoff for the Haleakala Highway (Route 37) but *don't take it* unless you're chasing a summit sunrise. Instead, continue past the airport along Route 36 a few more miles to **Lower Pa'ia**, an old sugar town taken over by windsurfers and their entourages. (Route 36 continues to Hana, see *Itinerary 16*.) Turn off and continue up towards Pa'ia – for breakfast, try **Charley's**. Further along is **Makawao**, a serious *paniolo* town settled by Portuguese immigrants working on area ranches. Its rough edges are softening with a scattering of new galleries, shops, and eateries.

Follow the signs for Haleakala. You're 'upcountry' now, on Haleakala's gentle slopes where the air is often brisk and the mood content. The final stretch of road, after zigzagging through Makawao and Pukalani, twists like a crazed serpent all the way to Haleakala's top, taking about an hour. The road could be slick, even icy, and sometimes wrapped in fog.

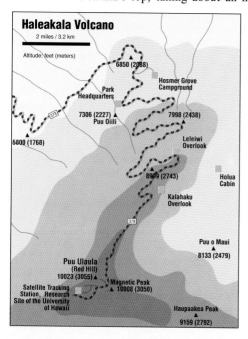

Haleakala National Park is the prize at road's end. The park encompasses the 19-sq mile (49-sq km), 3,000-ft (915-m) deep **Haleakala Crater**, plus Haleakala's eastern slope to the ocean. The crater view is simply breathtaking – further adjectives fail miserably and I won't try. On the opposite side 7 miles (11½ km) miles away is **Kipahulu Valley**, a nature preserve and rain forest closed to the public; the valley drops down Haleakala's east slope. Contemplate the crater from

Haleakala Crater

two lookouts: **Kalahaku** and **Pu'u Ula'ula**, at the summit. Feel the crater itself by hiking along some of its many miles of trails for an hour or for several days. Or take a horse down. Near the Pu'u Ula'ula summit lookout is a satellite tracking station tended by the federal government and the University of Hawaii. Don't try getting in, because it's closed to the public.

Although seemingly barren, Haleakala is refuge for two unique species: the remarkable silversword plant with their dagger-shaped silvery leaves and the nene goose. Related to the sunflower, silversword plants – Hawaii's official state flower and unique to the Hawaiian Islands – sometimes wait two decades or so before blooming just once before dying. Growing up to a height of 3 to 8ft (1 to 2½m), silverswords most commonly burst forth their flowers from June through October. The nene goose, once nearly ex-

Endangered crossing

tinct, lacks the webbed feet so essential for negotiating the craggy lava rock.

Powerful as Haleakala is on the mind and spirit, eventually you've got to come down along the same road. At the bottom, turn left onto Route 377 towards **Kula**. The climate here is nearly perfect for the strangely beautiful protea flower – you might stop at one of several protea farms in the Kula area. The **Kula Lodge** is good for a late breakfast. Follow Route 37 south as it narrows over an unquestionably idyllic countryside, more like Ireland or Kentucky than tropical Hawaii. Alalakeiki Channel lies ahead; you can see Kahoolawe, Lanai, Molokai, and a cute half moon islet called Molokini, which is a seabird sanctuary, marine conservation district, and popular snorkeling spot all in one. Long ago, during one of the ice ages when sea levels were 300ft (90m) lower, all these islands and Maui were one big island. Along South Maui's coast, the resorts of Wailea look rather tiny from this 3,000-ft (900-m) elevation. To the far left of Wailea, past Makena, is Maui's most recent lava flow, c. 1790.

Just past the rustic general store of Ulupalakua Ranch is the **Tedeschi Winery**, once the site of a sugar mill and since 1974 the only commercial winery in Hawaii, producing unique island brews like pineapple wine and Ulupalakua Red. Wine connoisseurs might raise their eyebrows, but I suggest you get a bottle or two for a

Tedeschi Winery

sunset picnic on the beach later. After a few minutes in the tasting room, a retired hundred-year-old jail, tour the winery and stretch your legs before heading back towards Kula.

Stay left on Route 37 towards Pukalani. In Pukalani, turn right to Makawao for an hour or two of browsing or eating. Try **Polli's** for Mexican food, or **Casanova Italian Restaurant**, which has a good takeout deli.

Rather than take the main road to Pa'ia, continue down to the coast on Route 400, a nice backcountry road. At the junction, left is Route 36, right is 360 – the Hana Highway. *Don't even think about a quick jaunt to Hana right now*, not unless you're spending the night in Hana. (See *Itinerary 16*.) Turn left and follow Route 36 along the coast towards Kahului. A few minutes before Pa'ia,

Late for the waves, Ho'okipa Beach

stop at **Ho'okipa Beach**, either at a lookout on one of the bluffs, or at the beach parking lot. Ho'okipa is a world-class windsurfing spot because of ideal waves and wind. On good days – for the diehard, that means every day – scores of windsurfers, many of them competitive professionals, ride the waves and wind.

It's probably late afternoon, and the remaining day is yours for what needs to be done: catching an inter-island flight, going for a sunset dip in clear Pacific waters, or checking out the fresh local products prepared in innovative fashion at **Haliimaile General Store.** Dinner options: **Mama's Fish House** near Ho'okipa Beach, pasta and live music at **Casanova's**, or uncork that wine over a picnic by the beach while plotting your next adventure. A return to Haleakala's summit for sunset is not that crazy of an idea, either.

Protea

16. Hana Highway

A day trip along the famous Hana Highway to the town of Hana and Ohe'o Gulch with its refreshing pools.

Forget the silly T-shirts trumpeting 'survival' of the **Hana Highway**. It's nonsense; locals commute on the highway everyday. Built by convicts over half a century ago, the Hana Highway is a fine road, narrow but paved and well-marked. There are, however, some tight curves that make for slow travel. Over 600 curves, by some counts, so drive carefully.

The road requires a full day round trip at minimum, and a full tank of gas at the start. If this is to be a day trip, then leave as early as possible. By late morning, traffic peaks. Returning, traffic is heavy in late afternoon. Plan on three to four hours, one way. You might easily do better, but enjoy yourself, for the road itself is the main attraction.

The Hana Highway takes off on its own where the road changes from Route 36 to 360, at the junction with Route 400 beyond Ho'okipa Beach. In Pa'ia, top off the gas tank and pick up a picnic lunch at **Picnics**; breakfasts are good here, too. Except for roadside fruit stands, the next food and gas stop is in Hana, where the pickings are either pricey or off the store shelf.

The highway's scenery is predictable: rich and lush forests, resplendent waterfalls at nearly every bend (or so it seems) and fine ocean vistas. Pleasant rest stops, now or on the return: **Waikamoi Ridge Trail Nature Walk**, **Kaumahina State Park**, and **Ke'anae Arboretum**. There's a dandy lookout above the small Hawaiian community of **Wailua**, nestled amidst cultivated taro. A must stop, just before Hana, is **Wai'anapanapa State Park**, with its black-sand beach and caves.

Hana itself is nearly anticlimactic after the drive. Rippling with quiet and unruffled serenity, there's hardly a touristy touch any-

End of the Hana Highway

Wailua nestles amidst cultivated taro

where, save the tourists themselves. The cross which commands the slopes above Hana honors Paul Fagan, who built the hotel and started the ranch in the 1940s.

Accommodations in Hana run the gamut. The **Hotel Hana-Maui** is an expensive, low-profile retreat favored by those who want privacy or just a fine meal. Other equally idyllic if more rustic accommodations include the **Heavenly Hana Inn** and **Aloha Cottages**. House rentals and a few cute bed and breakfasts are also on hand, or you can stay in one of the rustic state cabins at Wai'anapanapa. Whatever type of accommodation suits your style, plan ahead. Don't expect to find an empty room at the last minute.

The Hana Highway may lead to Hana, but there's more beyond. The road now deteriorates considerably but scenery expands exponentially. Beyond Hana is the lower extent of **Haleakala National Park**. From mid-morning until late afternoon, you won't be alone at **Ohe'o Gulch**, often erroneously called the 'Seven Sacred' Pools, of which they're neither. There are actually a couple dozen pools, filled by a stream coming down Haleakala. Only the lower pools near the ocean are ever crowded. Take the **Waimoku Falls Trail** to the upper pools for privacy. But later...

Wai'anapanapa Beach

ah, later, towards sunset, all the pools empty of people. Then they indeed feel sacred, if not heavenly.

At the pools' ocean outlet is a large grassy area ending abruptly on high ocean cliffs. The stone remains of a Hawaiian fishing village are nearby. Forget swimming in the ocean: dangerous currents and big sharks make the pools more inviting.

Beyond Hana

Whales

Visit Hawaii in winter and you'll have company: about 600 humpback whales down from the Arctic. Here to mate, give birth, and nurture newborn, whales like privacy – federal law requires a 300-ft (100-m) distance for whale watchers. The law is strictly enforced by arrest and fine, and occasionally imprisonment, as more than one European tourist has learned.

Having said that, definitely go whale watching, from the shore or from a boat. You can see whales anywhere, even off Diamond Head, but your safest bet is in the sheltered waters between Maui, Molokai, Lanai, and Kahoolawe. Don't worry about finding a whale-watching boat on Maui. They'll find you. I prefer the Captain Zodiac or Captain Nemo's excursions (see the *Activities* chapter), not exactly luxurious like the big boats, but sure adventure.

• *Whale watching season*: November through April, best around January.
• *How to know you've seen a whale*: when they spout – inhaling and exhaling on the surface – and when they fluke, spy hop, and breach.
• *Number of whales in Hawaii*: About 600, a mere fraction of a century ago.
• *Data*: 10–15ft (3½–4½m) long at birth, weighing 1–3 tons (1,016 –3,048kg). Newborns gain 200 lbs (90½kg) a day. Adults average 45ft (13½m) in length and 40 tons (40,642kg) in weight.

Rather than racing daylight back to Ka'anapali or Wailea at the end of the day, you might stay here until sundown, with the pools to yourself, followed by dinner at the Hotel Hana-Maui. Driving the road back at night is no problem – oncoming traffic, when and if there is any, is announced far ahead by headlights. And if a romantic moon smiles overhead, well, then...

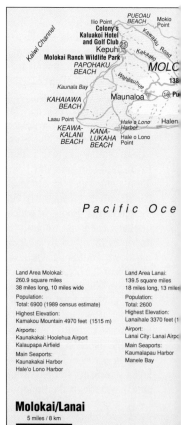

Land Area Molokai:
260.9 square miles
38 miles long, 10 miles wide
Population:
Total: 6900 (1989 census estimate)
Highest Elevation:
Kamakou Mountain 4970 feet (1515 m)
Airports:
Kaunakakai: Hoolehua Airport
Kalaupapa Airfield
Main Seaports:
Kaunakakai Harbor
Hale'o Lono Harbor

Land Area Lanai:
139.5 square miles
18 miles long, 13 miles
Population:
Total: 2600
Highest Elevation:
Lanaihale 3370 feet (1
Airport:
Lanai City: Lanai Airpo
Main Seaports:
Kaumalapau Harbor
Manele Bay

Molokai/Lanai

5 miles / 8 km

17. Molokai and Lanai

Within sight of Maui are Molokai and Lanai, two quiet and slow-paced islands ideal for a day or longer, by boat or by plane. Choose just one per day.

Thought by ancient Polynesians to be ghost stomping grounds and thus best avoided, **Lanai's** red volcanic earth later proved fertile for pineapples, long this privately-owned island's economic backbone. But the island's corporate owners are shedding pineapples for tourism. Two new luxury hotels have appeared on Lanai: the **Manele Bay Hotel** with a Mediterranean-Hawaiian ambiance, and **The Lodge at Koele**, with fireplaces and an Old World character. Accessible by plane and excursion boats from Maui, including half-day snorkeling trips, Lanai is the perfect place to do nothing – there are only a few dozen miles of pavement.

Larger and geographically more diverse, **Molokai** is a good island for exploration. It has wide open grasslands, moody rain forests, and on the north shore, the world's tallest ocean cliffs.

Tour operators infest Hawaii, and I shun them like I do rabid hounds. But there are two tours worth visiting Molokai alone for.

The first is the **Molokai Wagon Ride**, so unpretentious and so refreshingly local, operated by a trio of lifetime Molokai residents.

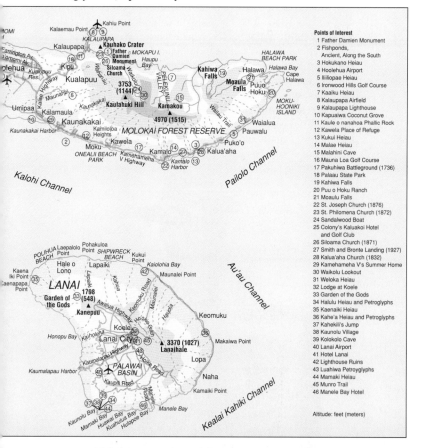

Points of Interest
1 Father Damien Monument
2 Fishponds,
   Ancient, Along the South
3 Hokukano Heiau
4 Hoolehua Airport
5 Iiiiliopae Heiau
6 Ironwood Hills Golf Course
7 Kaaiku Heiau
8 Kalaupapa Airfield
9 Kalaupapa Lighthouse
10 Kapuaiwa Coconut Grove
11 Kaule o nanahoa Phallic Rock
12 Kawela Place of Refuge
13 Kukui Heiau
14 Malae Heiau
15 Malahini Cave
16 Mauna Loa Golf Course
17 Pakuhiwa Battleground (1736)
18 Palaau State Park
19 Kahiwa Falls
20 Puu o Hoku Ranch
21 Moaula Falls
22 St. Joseph Church (1876)
23 St. Philomena Church (1872)
24 Colony's Kaluakoi Hotel
   and Golf Club
25 Colony's Kaluakoi Hotel
   and Golf Club
26 Siloama Church (1871)
27 Smith and Bronte Landing (1927)
28 Kalua'aha Church (1832)
29 Kamehameha V's Summer Home
30 Waikolu Lookout
31 Weloka Heiau
32 Lodge at Koele
33 Garden of the Gods
34 Halulu Heiau and Petroglyphs
35 Kaenaiki Heiau
36 Kahe'a Heiau and Petroglyphs
37 Kahekili's Jump
38 Kaunolu Village
39 Kolokolo Cave
40 Lanai Airport
41 Hotel Lanai
42 Lighthouse Ruins
43 Luahiwa Petroglyphs
44 Mamaki Heiau
45 Munro Trail
46 Manele Bay Hotel

Altitude: feet (meters)

Beach time, grilled fish, an immense heiau, anecdotes, history, culture, guitar music, fruit yanked from handy trees, and sincerity all along the way. Not to be missed.

The second tour humbles you with modern Hawaii's saddest but most graceful episode: the **former leprosy colony** on **Kalaupapa Peninsula**, isolated from the rest of Molokai by 2,000-ft (610-m) high cliffs and dangerous ocean waters. Starting in the early 1800s, Oahu health authorities shipped over 10,000 people – anybody with leprosy, now called Hansen's disease, and often those with nothing more than a bad skin rash – to Kalaupapa for a life sentence of exile. The first exiles were literally pushed off the boat and left to swim for the shore. The 1873 arrival of Joseph De Veuster from Belgium, better known as Father Damien, brought civility and dignity to Kalaupapa. He later contracted and died of Hansen's disease. Protected by the National Park Service, the community has about 100 voluntary patients and residents. You can fly to Kalaupapa, but better is hiking down the cliffs from 'topside.' All visitors require an escort; children under 16 are not allowed. Permission is required to visit Kalaupapa, obtained through airlines or local travel agents. If traveling independently, contact the state department of health in Honolulu or Molokai.

The best accommodation on Molokai is **Colony's Kaluakoi Hotel and Golf Club**, a low-key hotel that doesn't overwhelm its quiet west-end location. Also on Molokai's western end is the **Molokai Ranch Wildlife Park Safari**, where zebras, axis deer and giraffes inexplicably seem to fit in here. In Maunaloa, be sure to stop at the **Big Wind Kite Factory** for high-flying memories.

There are two must-dos on Molokai. **Papohaku Beach** stretches two miles long, and chances are that the only footprints you'll see there are your own. To the far east of the island is **Halawa Valley**, site of an old community dating back to AD650 and now lush with taro, ginger, guava and streams. The hike back to **Moaula Falls** is muddy but worth every step.

Father Damien

Eating Out

Hawaii's culinary offerings are bountiful, crossing over and blending into truly delightful experiences, like the increasingly-popular Pacific Rim cuisine. Yet one can also find pure ethnic food throughout the islands, especially from Asia and, of course, Italy. This listing is anything but comprehensive, and definitely not an effort to proclaim the *best* of Hawaii, for there are many more just as good, perhaps subjectively better. But these are all enjoyable in one way or another – for cuisine, presentation, atmosphere or experience. But like the stock marke and love affairs, restaurants have the ups and downs. Serious eaters shoul buy the Zagat Hawaii Restaurant Su vey, a little red book of restaurar evaluations. Three restaurant ho spots outside of Waikiki not covere below are Ward Center on Ala Moar Boulevard, Restaurant Row at A Moana and Punchbowl, and Aloh Tower Marketplace at Pier 10.

A general price guide for a meal fc two without drinks or tips is catego rized as follows: $ = under US$3($$ = US$30–$60, $$$ = over US$6(

Oahu

A LITTLE BIT OF SAIGON
1160 Maunakea Street, Chinatown
Tel: 528 3663
Nothing fancy except the food: exce lent and satisfying Vietnamese cuisir in a pleasant setting. $

ANDY'S (AKA MANOA HEALTH MARKE)
2904 East Manoa Road, Manoa Vall
Tel: 988 6161
Everything that Andy serves up fro dawn to dusk is satisfying, wheth its one of his healthy sandwiches ar salads, or the brownies and muffir Rustic seating. $

CAFE BRIO
Manoa Marketplace, Manoa Valley
Tel: 988 5555
Open and airy, with a well-receive pasta-and-Pacific Rim menu. $$

Imported cuisine

Andy's, Manoa Valley

CAFFÉLATTE
339 Saratoga Road, Waikiki
Tel: 924 1414
At a quiet end of Waikiki, with open-air seating. Perfectly-served home-made pasta with unpronounceable but perfect sauces. $$$

CASTAGNOLA'S ITALIAN LANAI
1920 Ala Moana Blvd, Waikiki
Tel: 949 6277
Casty's is an institution, albeit a busy one during peak hours. Regulars flock to this al fresco eatery for Italian food like Mama used to make. $$

HOKU
Kahala Mandarin Oriental
Tel: 734 2211
Chic multi-layer dining room with fish and seafood, steaks from a char-coal grill and wood-burning oven, and an oyster and sushi bar. $$$

KACHO
Waikiki Parc Hotel, Waikiki
Tel: 921 7272
Intimate Japanese restaurant with an emphasis on seafood and sushi. Fine Japanese dining requires serenity and imperceptible effort; Kacho excels at both. $$–$$$

KEO'S THAI CUISINE
625 Kapahulu Avenue
Tel: 737 8240
It's hard not to mention Keo's: cele-brities and locals drool over its Thai food. Keo's is part of an empire: there's another **Keo's** at Ward Cen-ter, and the original **Mekong**. $$–$$$

ORCHIDS
Halekulani Hotel, Waikiki
Tel: 923 2311
An outside restaurant open to the ocean and romance. Service and food is excellent, as is Sunday's brunch, but starve the night before. $$–$$$

PARC CAFE
Waikiki Parc Hotel, Waikiki
Tel: 921 7272
The Parc's buffet – especially dinner – is innovatively-prepared, and well-priced. Highly recommended. $$

ROY'S RESTAURANT
6600 Kalanianaole Highway
Hawaii Kai
Tel: 396 7697
One of Honolulu's most popular Hawaiian regional cuisine restau-rants. Problem: getting there through road-construction hell. $$–$$$

Big Island

ALOHA THEATER CAFE
Highway 11, Kainaliu
Tel: 322 3383
Diverse menu, from vegetarian to burg-ers to its decadent brownies. Best known for breakfasts outside on the terrace. $

CANOEHOUSE
Mauna Lani Bay Hotel & Bungalows
South Kohala
Tel: 885 6622
Has a reputation for its creative am-bience and Pacific Rim menu. Open-air seating. Superb sunsets. $$–$$$

Chinatown

Local Eats

To eat local and cheap without retreating to cheeseburgers, one must know what to ask for.

Dishes

bento: sometimes faithful to the Japanese original, sometimes localized beyond recognition. Great for picnics, with a little bit of everything: rice, pickled vegetables, meat or fish, and other curious things.

crackseed: seasoned seeds, including papaya, coconut, mango, pumpkin and watermelon.

huli huli chicken: if you drive past a park or grocery store parking lot and the air is filled with good-smelling smoke, it's huli huli chicken time – chicken cooked on a spit and sold in a bag.

malasada: from Portugal, much like a hole-less donut dipped in sugar.

manapua: Chinese steamed pastry with sweet pork and/or vegetables inside.

plate lunch: cheap and filling, with two scoop rice (*not* two scoops of rice) dished out with an ice cream scoop. A side scoop of macaroni salad, and some sort of meat on the rice. The variations are limitless and sometimes even interesting.

poi: pounded taro plant root, mixed with water into a thick paste. Said to be nutritious but it's something of, um, an acquired taste.

pupu: Called an hors d'oeuvre elsewhere,

pupus are properly eaten with a flower garnished tropical drink and a blossoming sunset on the horizon.

shave ice: those not in the know call these shaved ice, or worse, snow cones; this is akin to calling mousse a whipped pudding. Ice is shaved off a block in fine slivers, packed just right in a paper cone and topped with one or more sugar syrups. Connoisseurs request sweet *azuki* beans at the bottom, perhaps with vanilla ice cream, too.

saimin: looking like a bowl of noodles found anywhere in Asia, that's what it is, Hawaiian style. Includes fishcake, green onions, vegetables, maybe some bits of meat and other things in the broth.

Fish

ahi: yellowfin tuna. Widely used in Hawaii, including for sushi and sashimi.

aku: Skipjack tuna. Heavier than *ahi*.

mahimahi: dolphin gamefish, not the mammal. Ubiquitous in Hawaii, mild tasting and usually grilled or baked. So popular it often must be imported. Ask for fresh, not frozen.

ono: wahoo, or king mackerel. Seasonal in autumn and winter. Popular in most restaurants.

opakapaka: pink snapper. Used in upscale restaurants.

uku: grey or deep-sea snapper, excellent broiled, fried or baked.

JAMESON'S BY THE SEA
77–6452 Ali'i Drive, Kailua-Kona
Tel: 329 3195
Romantic and on the beach, nearly perfect seafood, especially local fish and smoked salmon. American fare too. Delicious setting at sunset. $$

LE SOLEIL
Mauna Lani Bay Hotel & Bungalows
South Kohala
Tel: 885 6622
Sophisticated and romantic French and Continental dinners. Outstanding wine list and attention to detail. Jacket required. $$$

MERRIMAN'S
Highway 19, Waimea
Tel: 885 6822
People drive and fly to Waimea for Merriman's incredible Pacific Rim and local menu. Highly-regarded throughout Hawaii. $$–$$$

RIYSSEK'S
60 Keawe Street, Hilo
Tel: 935 5111
With its authentic Cajun-Creole menu, Roussel's would be a great surprise, anywhere. Lunch or dinner in a beautifully restored building. $$–$$$

SIBU CAFE
75–5695 Ali'i Drive, Kona
Tel: 329 1112
Purveyor of good Southeast Asian dishes, without pretense. Popular for its Indonesian food and ambience. $

Kauai

A PACIFIC CAFE
4831 Kuhio Highway, Kapa'a
Tel: 822 0013
Consistently receives high marks from locals, even competitors. Prices match its upscale but easy-going surroundings. Asian and Pacific Rim food. $$–$$$

BRENNECKE'S BEACH BROILER
2100 Hoone Road, Poipu Beach
Tel: 742 7588
Across the street from the beach and on the mark for food – seafood, beef, burgers and a big salad bar. A solid venue for people and sunset watching. Beach sandals required. $–$$

CASA DI AMICI
2484 Keneke Road, Kilauea
Tel: 828 1388
Worth a drive for dinner, this nice little restaurant has well-prepared pasta topped with a wide variety of sauces. Open-air seating, with intimate music in the evenings. $$

GAYLORD'S
Kilohana, in Puhi
Tel: 245 9593
In an open courtyard at a 1930s estate mansion, Gaylord's is a requisite stop on a culinary tour of the islands. Somewhat pricey menu. $$–$$$

THE GROVE
Waimea Plantation Cottages, Waimea
Tel: 338 2300
Tables on the dining lanai make the most of The Grove's 1930s plantation mood. Steaks, burgers and seafood. $$

A delicately strung lei

LA CASCATA
Princeville Hotel, near Hanalei
Tel: 826 2761
Mediterranean atmosphere, right
down to the tall windows that swing
open to the outside. Its fine cuisine
extends considerably beyond the usual
pasta. Romantic. $$$

SINALOA TAQUERIA
1-3959 Kaumualii Highway, Hanapepe
Tel: 335 0006
Dubbed 'the best authentic Mexican
food on Kauai,' it's run by chefs from
south of the border. Known for its
bright, cheery interiors and a salsa
that doesn't quit. $

Maui

AVALON RESTAURANT
844 Front Street, Lahaina
Tel: 667 5559
A Pacific/Asian menu of eclectic di-
versity and excellence makes this court-
yard restaurant an 'in' place for the
hungry and the knowing. $$

THE BAY CLUB
Kapalua Bay Hotel & Villas
West Maui
Tel: 669 5656
A contender for Hawaii's most-ro-
mantic setting category. Oceanfront
vistas, plus excellent service and food,
make lunch and dinner here among
Maui's best. Jacket for dinner. $$–$$$

CASANOVA ITALIAN RESTAURANT
1188 Makawao Avenue, Makawao
Tel: 572 0220
Pastas and a wood-fired oven that
coughs out excellent pizzas. A deli is
open all day. Live music and dancing
at night. $$

DAVID PAUL'S LAHAINA GRILL
Lahaina Hotel,
127 Lahainaluna Road, Lahaina
Tel: 667 5117

This beautifully renovated place is
among the best and most in vogue
Innovative Pacific Rim menu. Sophis-
ticated but relaxed. $$–$$$

GERARD'S
The Plantation Inn,
174 Lahainaluna Road, Lahaina
Tel: 661 8939
Expensive and chic, romantic and re-
laxing – there's pleasure in its wide-
ranging French cuisine. Outdoor seat-
ing on the lanai, or indoors. $$–$$$

LONGHI'S
888 Front Street, Lahaina
Tel: 667 2288
Eccentric for its walking-and-talking
menus, Longhi's once-trendy chicness
now has a solid reputation, including
people-watching. American and Ital-
ian fare. $$

MAMA'S FISH HOUSE
Highway 36, Kuau, near Pa'ia
Tel: 579 8488
One of those places that excels without trumpeting its success. A wonderful spot right on the ocean, it has
what some say, Maui's best fish. Those
in the know, go. $$–$$$

THE PACIFIC GRILL
Four Seasons Resort, Wailea,
South Maui
Tel: 874 8000
Breakfast, lunch and dinner – there's
simply nothing less than perfect here.
Perhaps the best of Pacific Rim menus,
and ocean views, too. $$–$$$

SAENG'S THAI CUISINE
2119 Vineyard Street, Wailuku
Tel: 244 1568
Thai food in a bright, quiet ambience, especially in the garden. Food
and service is excellent. Nearby is
Siam Thai Cuisine, with good food
but lacking in atmosphere. $$

Shopping

Like eating, shopping is surely subjective. Some people flourish in large shopping centers and malls, others shrivel up within sight of one. Hawaii has huge shopping malls and small boutiques to suit all tastes. The island itineraries have high-lighted some of the places to go, others are listed below.

There are a few things that make uniquely Hawaiian gifts, disregarding cheap souvenirs of baseball caps and coffee cups. The following are some of the more interesting ones:

Scrimshaw: the engraving of a polished bone or ivory surface with a sharp, pointed tool. Ink is then spread over the surface and absorbed only in the engraved lines. The result is a cross between an etching and tattoo. The art came into its own in the 1800s when bored sailors on whaling vessels scratched pictures on whale teeth. A number of non-endangered materials are now used, such as fossilized walrus tusk. The best buys are on Maui, in Lahaina and Ka'anapali.

Kona coffee: Mark Twain liked Kona coffee, as I do. The Kona coffee plants originally came from Rio de Janeiro in the early 1800s. The plant grew well in several places in Hawaii, but flourished in South Kona, on the Big Island, which is where the only commercially-grown coffee in America now grows. It takes 500lb

Waikiki window shopping

more upscale place but still retaining a strong local flavor with many of the older stores. Open-air and huge, with some 200 shops. Monday to Saturday, 9.30am to 9pm; Sunday, 10am to 5pm.

WARD CENTRE
1200 Ala Moana Boulevard,
near Ala Moana Park
Tel: 591 8411
High class and upscale, with nearly three dozen shops and restaurants, most of them excellent and with a wide range of cuisines. Good place to wander around evenings. Open Monday to Friday, 10am to 9pm; Saturday, 10am to 5pm; Sunday, 11am to 4pm.

WARD WAREHOUSE
1050 Ala Moana Boulevard
Tel: 591 8411
Inviting and casual, with a wide range of stores and cheap eats. About 70 shops in this open-air shopping center. Open Monday to Friday, 10am to 9pm; Saturday, 10am to 5pm; Sunday, 11am to 4pm.

ROYAL HAWAIIAN SHOPPING CENTER
2201 Kalakaua Avenue, Waikiki
Tel: 922 0588
This large open-air mall is Waikiki's biggest with more than 150 stores. Difficult to miss, located just between the Royal Hawaiian Hotel and Kalakaua Avenue. Good for wandering if not buying. Open daily 9am to 10pm, Sunday to 9pm.

INTERNATIONAL MARKET PLACE
2330 Kalakaua Avenue, Waikiki,
across from Moana Hotel.
Outdoors and casual. Bargaining is acceptable for anything and everything from gold jewelry and clothes to souvenirs and food. Casual restaurants. Open daily, 9am until midnight or later.

(227kg) of coffee beans to make 100lb (45kg) of processed coffee. Freshest on the Kona Coast, but sold throughout Hawaii at about the same prices.
Niihau shell lei: Niihau is a small, dry island west of Kauai. Privately owned by the wealthy Robinson family of Kauai, the island is used mostly for ranching. A small community of about 250 Hawaiians live on the island, where Hawaiian is the language of education and the daily life of the people. Niihau is *kapu* to visitors, ie off limits. Residents there collect small, rare shells washed onto the beach and string them into necklaces of delicate colors. Very expensive. Best bought on Kauai at upscale galleries and jewelry stores.

Shopping Centres
Oahu

ALA MOANA CENTER
Ala Moana Boulevard, between Waikiki
and downtown Honolulu
Tel: 946 2811
This is *the* shopping center in all of Hawaii. Recently renovated into a

Hanapepe window shopping

Kauai

KILOHANA
Route 50, 2 miles west of Lihue
Tel: 245 5608
Plantation estate with select retail shops and galleries. If there's time for only one shopping excursion, this is best. Open daily 9am.

COCONUT MARKETPLACE
Between Wailua River and Kapa'a, 15 mins north of Lihue
Tel: 822 3641
Standard shopping mall with 70 outdoor shops. Open daily 9am to 9pm.

Maui

WHALERS VILLAGE
Kaanapali Beach
Tel: 661 4567
Over 50 shops, and a whaling museum. Outdoors – it's right on the beach among the resort hotels. Open daily 9.30am to 10pm

LAHAINA CANNERY MALL
1221 Honoapiilani Highway, north end of Lahaina
Tel: 661 5304
Standard shopping mall of about 50 shops. Convenient location at West Maui. Open daily 9.30am to 9.30pm.

Big Island

PRINCE KUHIO PLAZA
111 E. Puainako Street, Hilo 96720
Tel: 959 3555
Largest enclosed mall on the Big Island. Monday to Wednesday, Saturday, 9.30am to 5.30pm; Thursday and Friday, 9.30am to 9pm: Sunday, 10am to 4pm

PARKER SQUARE SHOPPING MALL
Route 19, Waimea
Tel: 885 7178
Small stores and boutiques, but most interesting is the **Gallery of Great Things**, open 9am to 5pm, with island crafts – lots of wood – and art.

Whalers Village at Kaanapali Beach, Maui

Activities

BEACHES

It's impossible to list all of Hawaii's beaches. Those that follow are but a few of many nice ones. Not all are necessarily good swimming beaches, but there's more to a beach than just swimming – sunbathing, scenery and people-watching come to mind.

Coral injuries, even the small nip, infect easily and heal slowly. If there is reason to worry about sharks, you'll know. Don't turn your back on waves, especially in winter. Windward beaches sometimes have jellyfish invasions; watch for golf-ball-size, purplish man-of-wars on the sand and in the water. Finally, Hawaii's beaches undergo radical personality changes from season to season. North shore beaches are usually glass-smooth in summer, but viciously rough in winter. Use your head, follow the warnings, and ask the lifeguard.

Oahu

Sandy Beach: Fantastic sun, sand setting, and people watching. But the water is always unpredictable, seasonally dangerous. *Always check with lifeguards*, even when people are in the water; they're probably expert body surfers, and Sandy's their turf. Full facilities.

Waimanalo: Safe beach all year, with lush and dramatic scenery. One of Hawaii's longest beaches, with a gentle, shallow bottom. Weekdays the beach is nearly always empty; weekends bring out the canoe clubs, baseball practice, and families. Full facilities and picnic areas.

Kailua Beach: Not easy to find, but well-known. A good recreational beach with excellent swimming, windsurfing, but so-so snorkeling. Safe all year, with a nice sandy bottom that slopes gently.

Malaekahana: Not so popular, not

Waimanalo Beach

Ka'anapali Parade

so typical but quite a beautiful beach. Large groves of ironwood trees, with campgrounds and full facilities. The water is usually calm, clear, and excellent for swimming, especially for children.

Waimea Bay: Glass-smooth in summer for perfect swimming and snorkeling – but come winter, the bay is explosive and suitable only for world-class surfers. A small but beautiful beach; full facilities and lifeguards. Exciting in winter, sleepy in summer.

Big Island

Spencer Beach Park: In the shadow of a powerful temple to the war god, this is a popular local beach, perfect for families with children; snorkeling and swimming are good, but of course, the sunsets are better. Full facilities.

Kauna'oa Beach, aka Mauna Kea Beach Resort: A graceful crescent of sand, this is one of the Big Island's finest beaches. Although the Mauna Kea Hotel dominates it, the beach is public, with showers and restrooms at the southern end. Great swimming and snorkeling.

Hapuna Beach: A long white sand beach that would be excellent on any island, but on this beach-short island, Hapuna is stupendous. Full facilities. Sun is guaranteed anytime except night. Full picnicking and camping facilities. Good for winter whale watching.

Kealakekua Bay: Not much of a beach here, but adequate. Historically the area is interesting: a heiau hunkers nearby and Captain Cook made his final splash down the way. The bay is a state underwater park, meaning it has good snorkeling. Facilities.

Kauai

Polihale: Kauai's remotest beach but still easily reached by car – just drive to the end of the road. This is the western end of the Na Pali Coast, and the cliffs that flank the beach's northeast end are impressive. Wild – use common sense. Facilities, no lifeguard.

Poipu: Good play area: swimming, snorkeling, picnics, sand castles. Bodysurfers thrive at nearby Brennecke Beach. Close to the resorts and thus sometimes crowded. The Poipu Beach area is quite nice and beautiful, good area for children. Full facilities.

Hanalei: Kauai's best beaches are on the north shore, not always swimmable but always spectacular and moody. Hanalei Bay Beach is wide and arcing, seeming to continue forever. Summer swimming is excellent, winter is dangerous and best avoided.

Lumaha'i: Often photographed from an overlook, this North Shore beach is better experienced down on the sand, where filming for *South Pacific* took place. The safest swimming spot is on the Hanalei Bay side; the currents here are tricky. No lifeguards.

Ha'ena/Ke'e: Used for the mystical Bali Hai in the film *South Pacific*. Most of the time, forget swimming at Ha'ena, but take in the scenery. Ke'e Beach, at the end of the road, is good for swimming and snorkeling in summer. Winters – uncork the wine and watch the pounders.

Maui

Kapalua: This beach is a simply superb beach, almost perfect in many ways, with good snorkeling and relaxing. A local favorite. Facilities. There can be some confusion with Fleming Beach nearby.

Ka'anapali: Maui's most famous beach and resort area. Three miles of fine sand and good swimming. But watch for the red flags signalling dangerous conditions. Has a sandy bottom that drops quickly. Good place to strut.

Wailea: Encompasses a series of beaches – Keawakapu, Mokapu, Ulua, and Wailea. Smooth and sandy bottoms. Public facilities are not always handy, but the sun certainly is. Ulua Beach is probably the most popular, with good bodysurfing, snorkeling. Up the coast in Kihei, **Kama'ole Beaches I, II,** and **III** are superb.

Ho'okipa: On the opposite coast from Maui's great resort beaches, this is a beach with great spectator activity world-class windsurfing. Swimming occasionally good. Full facilities including grills and picnic areas.

Hamoa: On the Hana end of Maui Hamoa is small but compactly elegant, buttressed by high cliffs and continual surf. Often strong currents right at the beach. No public facilities, but the Hotel Hana-Maui maintains facilities for guests and a lifeguard.

GOLF

Hawaii is peppered with dozens of golf courses, and more are coming. This is just a partial listing, of course. Hawaii's golf courses are popular with North Americans and Asians year round. Plan ahead. A spontaneous urge for a quick round of golf will usually leave the golfer practicing his or her swing on the beach, not so bad but not quite golf. Two sources of comprehensive information available in the bookshops are *Hawaii Golf Map* and the *Hawaii Golf Guide*.

Information is listed in this order: *number of holes, par, clubhouse (C), driving range (DR), approximate fees ($ = under US$40; $$ = US$40–$80; $$$ = over US$80), and Golf Digest rating.* All listed courses are public. The latest *Golf Digest* ratings of Hawaii golf courses are in:

1. Prince Golf and Country Club, Princeville, Kauai
2. Kauai Lagoons Resort, Lihue, Kauai
3. Mauna Kea Beach Golf Club, South Kohala, Big Island
4. Waikoloa Kings Course, South Kohala, Big Island
5. Princeville Makai Golf Course, Princeville, Kauai
6. Kapalua Golf Club (Village Course), Kapalua, West Maui
7. Kapalua Golf Club (Bay Course), Kapalua, West Maui

Kailua Beach

8. Sheraton Makaha Resort, West Oahu
9. Ko Olina Golf Club, West Oahu
0. Waialae Country Club, Honolulu, Oahu (private club)

Big Island

Hilo Municipal Golf Course
Hilo Tel: 959 7711
18 71 DR $

Mauna Kea Beach Golf Club
South Kohala Tel: 882 7222
18 72 C DR $$$ GD: #3

Mauna Lani Resort
South Kohala Tel: 885 6655
Two courses: 18 72/72 C DR $$$

Naniloa Country Club
Hilo Tel: 935 3000
9 35 C DR $

Volcano Golf and Country Club
Volcano Tel: 967 7331
18 72 C $$

Waikoloa Beach Golf Club
South Kohala Tel: 885 6060
18 70 C DR $$$

Waikoloa Kings Course
South Kohala Tel: 885 4647
18 72 C DR $$$ GD: #4

Maui and Molokai

Kapalua Golf Club
West Maui Tel: 669 8044
Three courses: 18 72/72/73 DR $$$
GD: #6 and #7

Makena Golf Club
South Maui Tel: 879 3344
18 72 C DR $$$

Ka'anapali Golf Course
West Maui Tel: 661 3691
Two courses: 18 72/72 DR $$$

Waiehu Municipal Golf Course
Wailuku, West Maui Tel: 244 5934
18 72 DR $$

Wailea Golf Club
South Maui Tel: 879 2966
Two courses: 72/72 C DR $$$

Kaluakoi Golf Club
Molokai Island Tel: 552 2739
18 72 C DR $$

Oahu

Ala Wai Golf Course
Honolulu Tel: 734 3656
18 70 C DR $
Note: world's busiest course according to the Guinness Book of Records.

Hawaii Kai Golf Course
East Honolulu Tel: 395 2358
Two courses: 18 72/55 C DR $$

Ko Olina Golf Club
West Oahu Tel: 676 5309
18 72 C DR $$$ GD: #9

Makaha Valley Country Club
West Oahu Tel: 695 9578
18 71 DR $$

Olomana Golf Links
Waimanalo Tel: 259 7926
18 72 C DR $

Sheraton Makaha Resort and Country Club
West Oahu Tel: 695 9544
18 72 DR $$$ GD: #8

Turtle Bay Hilton and Country Club
North Shore Tel: 293 8574
18 72 C DR $$$

Kauai

Kauai Lagoons Resort
Lihue Tel: 245 5061
Two courses: 18 72/72 C DR $$$
GD: #2

Kiahuna Golf Club
Poipu Tel: 742 9595
18 70 C DR $$

Poipu Bay Resort Golf Course
Poipu Tel: 742 9489
18 72 C DR $$

Prince Golf & Country Club
Princeville/North Shore Tel: 826 5000
18 72 C DR $$$ GD: #1

Princeville Makai Golf Course
Princeville/North Shore Tel: 826 3580
Three courses: 27 72 C DR $$
GD: #5

Wailua Municipal Golf Course
Kapa'a Tel: 245 8092
18 72 C DR $

OTHER ACTIVITIES

Raft Excursions

Kauai and Big Island

Captain Zodiac Raft Expeditions
P.O. Box 456, Hanalei 96714
Toll: (800) 422 7824
Kauai: Tel: 826 9371
Big Island: Tel: 329 3199
Motorized raft excursions, half a day
to a full day, on Kauai and the Big
Island is a pleasant experience. Cap-
tain Zodiac is the original but there
are other reliable companies too.
Pregnant women and those with bad
backs are usually excluded. Includes
lunch and snorkel equipment.

Diving

Some dive shops are like factories: On
Oahu, a lot of them are found in the
Waikiki area, catering mainly to
tourists. The shops listed here cater
to both locals and tourists, and are
generally a cut above others in both
service and quality. There are other
good shops, of course.

Kauai

Fathom Five Divers Tel: 742 6991
Kauai Sea Sports Tel: 742 9303

Oahu

Aaron's Dive Shop Tel: 262 2333
South Pacific Scuba Tel: 735 7196

Big Island

Kona Coast Divers Tel: 329 8802
Big Island Divers Tel: 329 6068

Maui

Lahaina Divers Tel: 661 4505
Capt Nemo's Tel: 661 5555

Submarines

An alternative to floating on the wa
ter or learning how to scuba dive is
submarine ride. **Atlantis** offers hour
long trips to depths of (46m) in 65-
(20-m) long, 80-ton (81,280kg) sub
marines with a capacity of 46 passen
gers and 3 crew. Large, 21-in (53-cm
diameter windows. Electric-powered.

Oahu

Departs hourly 7am to 5pm from
Hilton Hawaiian Village, Waikiki
Tel: 973 9811

Maui

Departs hourly from Pioneer Inn,
Lahaina. Tel: 667 2224

Big Island

Departs hourly from King Kame
hameha Hotel, Kona. Tel: 329 6626

Helicopters

Helicopter trips fly over wilderness
areas; there is controversy regarding
the noise intrusion for residents on
the ground. If you choose to fly any
way, the experience is superb. Hawaii
is swamped with helicopters; listed
here are reliable operators. **Kenai He
licopters** flies on several islands; sin
gle-island operators are just as good.

Helicopter, lava and ocean

Big Island

Mauna Kea Helicopters Tel: 885 6400
Volcano Heli-Tours Tel: 967 7578

Kauai

Bruce Needham Helicopters
Tel: 335 3115 Toll: (800) 359 3057
Ohana Helicopter Tours
Tel: 245 3996 Toll: (800) 222 6989

Maui

Blue Hawaiian Helicopters
Tel: 871 8844 Toll: (800) 247 5444
Sunshine Helicopters
Tel: 871 0722 Toll: (800) 544 2520
Hawaii Helicopters
Tel: 877 3900 Toll: (800) 346 2403

All Islands

Kenai Helicopters Hawaii
Toll: (800) 622 3144
Maui: Tel: 871 6463
Big Island: Tel: 329 7424
Kauai: Tel: 245 8591

Gliders

Oahu

Soar Hawaii North Shore, Oahu
Tel: 637 3147
The Original Glider Rides
North Shore, Oahu Tel: 677 3404

Walking Tours

Oahu

Passport Hawaii Tel: 943 0371.
A 2½-hour walking tour of old
Waikiki, peppered with ancient lore;
stories of romance, crimes, ghosts and
literary history. Highly recommended.
Saturday 9am. Meet at Duke Kahanamoku Statue, Kalakaua Avenue, Diamond Head side of Moana Hotel.

Four Wheel Drive Tours

Big Island

Waipi'o Valley Shuttle
P.O. Box 5128, Kukuihaele 96727
Tel: 775 7121
Four-wheel-drive tour of **Waipi'o
Valley**. Daily, allow 2-3 hours. Also:
Four-wheel-drive tours of **Mauna
Kea**, including telescope tour when
it's open. Full day.

Museums

Oahu

Bishop Museum
1525 Bernice Street, Honolulu 96817
Tel: 847 3511
Daily 9am to 5pm. Planetarium daily
11am, 2pm, and Friday, Saturday 7pm.

Contemporary Museum of Art
2411 Makiki Heights Drive
Honolulu Tel: 526 0232
Daily 10am to 4pm, Sun noon to 4pm.

Honolulu Academy of Arts
900 S. Beretania Street, Honolulu
Tel: 538 1006
Tuesday to Saturday 10am to 4.30pm,
Sunday 1 to 5pm.

Hawaii Maritime Center
Pier 7, Honolulu Harbor, Honolulu
Tel: 536 6373
Daily 9am to 5pm.

Big Island

Kamuela Museum
Junction of Routes 19 and 250,
Waimea
Tel: 885 4724
Open daily 8am to 5pm

Lyman Museum and Mission House
276 Haili Street, Hilo
Tel: 935 5021
Open Monday to Saturday 9am to
5pm, Sunday 1 to 4pm

Kauai

Kauai Museum
4428 Rice Street, Lihue 96766
Tel: 245 6931
Open Monday to Friday 9am to
4.30pm, Saturday 9am to 1pm.

Maui

Whalers Village Museum
Whalers Village Shopping Complex
2435 Kaanapali Parkway,
Lahaina 96761
Tel: 661 5992
Located in the Kaanapali resort area
Open daily 9.30am to 10pm.

Street critics, Lahaina

Nightlife

Perhaps I'm old-fashioned, but my idea of nightlife in Hawaii is romance on the beach, by starlight or moonlight, and a bottle of wine, with no sounds but the roll of the ocean and the liquid poetry of my sweet talk. But if you need something more, here are some suggestions for shows and dancing. Outside of Honolulu, the pickings are thin, at least by mainland standards. After all, there are all those beaches...

Oahu

HONOLULU COMEDY CLUB
Aston Waikiki Terrace Hotel,
2045 Kalakaua Avenue, Waikiki
Tel: 922 5998
National and local comedians. Has branch clubs on the neighboring islands; call for schedules and locations. Sometimes there's a sunset cruise comedy venue. Nightly.

FRANK DE LIMA
Outrigger Reef Towers Hotel,
227 Lewers Street, Waikiki
Tel: 923 9861
Very talented, very funny, very irreverent comedian. Popular with locals, cutting nobody any slack. De Lima sometimes shares the stage with guest artistes. The dinner show is highly recommended, but make reservations in advance. Nightly, from Tuesday to Saturday, 9pm.

ALOHA TOWER MARKETPLACE
Piers 8, 9 and 10 at Aloha Tower,
Honolulu
Tel: 528 5700
With dozens of bars and restaurants, this is Honolulu's hippest hangout.

Dusk falls on Waikiki

Most popular is the Gordon Biersch microbrewery, which has live outdoor music on the weekends. Call the hotline for information on evening events.

THE BROTHERS CAZIMERO
Bishop Museum, 1525 Bernice Street,
Honolulu Tel: 847 6353

95

Classic singers doing classic Hawaiian tunes. A dozen albums to their credit. Picnic supper from 5 to 6pm; self-guided museum tours until showtime at 7.30pm on Wednesday, Thursday and Sunday.

HOUSE WITHOUT A KEY
Halekulani Hotel, Waikiki
Tel: 923 2311
Outdoor lounge and patio at the Halekulani Hotel, Waikiki. Hawaiian favorites by the *Islanders*, on steel guitar and ukulele, accompanied by a former Miss Hawaii hula dancer.

STUDEBAKER'S
500 Ala Moana Boulevard
Tel: 531 8444
Several trendy and diverse restaurants and bars in this area. A place to see and be seen. Most popular is Studebaker's – a bar and classic-rock disco at night. Daily until 2am.

ANNA BANNANA'S
2440 South Beretania Street, Honolulu
Tel: 946 5190
Hip hangout for years with energetic bands, from reggae to rock 'n' roll. Near the University of Hawaii, and thus young crowds. Dancing and no dress code. Live music 9pm to 2am.

WAVE WAIKIKI
1877 Kalakaua Avenue, Honolulu
Tel: 941 0424
Long-time pop music venue for local and visiting bands. Dancing or drinking. Daily, 9pm to 4am.

Big Island

LEHUA'S BAY CITY BAR & GRILL
11 Waianuenue Avenue, Hilo
Tel: 935 8055
Indeed a bar and grill, Lehua's is also Hilo's zippiest place at night. Changing schedule of nightly jazz, dancing, and stand-up comedy.

ECLIPSE RESTAURANT
75–5711 Kuakini Hwy, Kailua
Tel: 329 4686
The disco tunes start up at 10pm Friday through Sunday.

Kauai

LEGENDS NIGHTCLUB
Pacific Ocean Plaza, 3501 Rice Street near Nawiliwili Harbor and the Kaua Marriott Resort
Tel: 246 0491
Kauai's largest dance floor. Live music, nightly specials; dancing and drinks from 8pm to 4am nightly.

GILLIGAN'S
Outrigger Kauai Beach Hotel, Lihue
Tel: 245 1955
Upscale resort action for music and dancing. Dress code. Sundays to Thursdays, 8pm to 2am, Friday and Saturday, 8pm to 4am.

Maui

TSUNAMI
Grand Wailea Resort Hotel & Spa, South Maui
Tel: 875 1234
The name says it all: tidal wave. High-class, high-power music and dancing in Wailea. Call for hours.

BLACKIE'S BAR
Blackie's Boat Yard, Route 30 near Lahaina Tel: 667 7979
A little eccentric, but well-known and very popular, especially for its jazz music. Food and drinks. Jazz on Monday, Wednesday, Friday and Sunday, 5.30 to 8.30pm.

MOOSE MCGILLYCUDDY'S
844 Front Street, Lahaina
Tel: 667 7758
There's lots of nightlife in Lahaina, but when it comes to dancing, the Moose reigns supreme. Good sandwiches, burgers and salads too.

Luaus

Luaus range from the tacky to the nearly authentic. But, like most first-time visitors to Hawaii, you'll probably have fun at any, or all, of them. Most resort hotels organize some sort of luau night with entertainment or a Polynesian revue. Advance reservations are required. Luaus are expensive, from US$40–$50 per adult – but you won't eat for a week afterwards, making it a real bargain. Because of their small size and reasonable authenticity, the following luaus are good bets:

Oahu

PARADISE COVE
West Oahu, Tel: 973 LUAU
Nightly 5.30pm

ROYAL HAWAIIAN LUAU
Royal Hawaiian Hotel, Waikiki
Tel: 923 7311
Mondays 6pm.

Big Island

KONA VILLAGE RESORT
South Kohala, Big Island
Tel: 885 6789
Fridays 6.15pm

Kauai

KAUAI COCONUT BEACH RESORT
Kapaa, Kauai Tel: 822 3455
Nightly except Wednesday and Friday.

TAHITI NUI
Hanalei, North Shore, Kauai
Tel: 826 6277
Wednesday and Friday, 6.30pm.

Maui

RENNAISANCE WAILEA BEACH RESORT
Wailea, South Maui, Tel: 879 4900
Thursdays, 6pm.

OLD LAHAINA LUAU
505 Front Street, Lahaina, Maui
Tel: 667 1998
Nightly, 5.30pm.

Lucky guy at Paradise Cove (the boss, actually)

Calendar of Special Events

JANUARY

Third week: Narcissus Queen Pageant. Held in Honolulu, this is part of the **Narcissus Festival**, continuing throughout February. A celebration of the Chinese New Year; includes a pageant, a coronation ball, Chinese cultural demonstrations and festivities with lion dances and food. Tel: 533 3181.

Third week: Annual Ala Wai Canoe Challenge. A no-experience-necessary canoe race down the Ala Wai Canal, Waikiki. Tel: 923 1802.

FEBRUARY

Continuation of **Narcissus Festival**, from January.

Third week: Annual Buffalo's Big Board Surfing Classic. Indeed a classic, with old-timers competing on old-fashioned wooden surfboards – the big boards. Hawaiian entertainment and food. Makaha Beach, Oahu. Tel: 525 8090.

Third week: Waimea Town Celebration. A big two-day town party with the usual festivities: food, entertainment, parade, games, races. Waimea, Kauai. Tel: 338 9957.

MARCH

First week: Cherry Blossom Festival. A Japanese cultural celebration held at Kapiolani Park, Waikiki. Includes traditional and contemporary Japanese entertainment, demonstrations, and mochi (rice) pounding. Tel: 949 2255

Variable: Hawaii Ski Cup Open. International and club snow ski races. The date depends on snow conditions. On the top of Mauna Kea, Big Island. Tel: 737 4394.

Last week: Prince Kuhio Festival. A celebration of Prince Jonah Kuhio Kalanianaole. Canoe races, royal ball, pageant, period music and dances, and a commemorative service. At Prince Kuhio Park, Poipu, Kauai. Tel: 245 3971. Also on other islands.

March 26: Prince Kuhio Day. State holiday in honor of Prince Jonah Kuhio Kalanianaole.

APRIL

Easter: Merrie Monarch Festival. The best of all the hula competitions, which concludes a week of celebration in honor of King Kalakaua. Hilo, on the Big Island. Tel: 935 9168. Alert: Hotel rooms are nearly impossible to book at the last minute in Hilo during the festival so make sure that you plan way ahead.

MAY

First week: Annual Lei Day Celebration. Cultural shows by elementary school students, statewide lei competitions, exhibitions and the Lei Queen coronation. Kapiolani Park, Waikiki. Tel: 266 7654. Celebrations also held on the neighboring islands.

JUNE

First and second week: King Kame-hameha Celebrations. Statewide festivities honoring Hawaii's first monarch. Includes the lei-draping ceremony of King Kamehameha statues in Honolulu and the Big Island, and parades and demonstrations.
June 11: Kamehameha Day. A state holiday.

JULY

Variable: Annual Makawao Rodeo and Parade. Probably the best of all Hawaii rodeos, and certainly its liveliest. Makawao, Maui. Tel: 572 9928.
Third week: Hale'iwa Bon Odori Festival. A cheerful Buddhist festival of the dead. Bon dances and a floating lantern ceremony. Highly recommended. Tel: 637 4382.
Third week: Kapalua Wine Symposium. Experts gather for seminars and tasting. Kapalua Bay Hotel, West Maui. Tel: 669 0244.
Third and fourth week: Koloa Plantation Days. A week of festivities celebrating the start of sugar plantations in Hawaii. Koloa, Kauai. Tel: 332 9201.

AUGUST

Variable: Annual Hawaiian International Billfish Tournament. The premier international marlin fishing contest. Kailua-Kona, Big Island. Tel: 836 0974.

First week: Queen Lili'uokalani Keiki Hula Competition. Young boys and girls from hula schools compete in both modern and ancient hula. Oahu. Tel: 521 6905.

SEPTEMBER

Last week through October: Aloha Festivals. In honor of the times of the Hawaiian monarchy with street parties, canoe races and parades. Dates vary widely from island to island. Tel: 944 8857.

OCTOBER

Variable: Ironman Triathlon World Championships. *The* race of the world: 2½-mile swim, 112-mile bicycle ride, and a 26-mile run. Kailua-Kona, Big Island Tel: 329 0063.

NOVEMBER

Variable, through December: Triple Crown of Surfing. Concludes the professional world tour of surfing. North Shore, Oahu. Tel: 377 5850.
Variable, through December: Hawaii International Film Festival. Showcases the best of films from throughout Asia, the Pacific, and the Americas. Tel: 944 7707.

DECEMBER

Second week: Annual Honolulu Marathon. International competitors gather in Oahu. Tel: 734 7200.

Practical Information

GETTING THERE

By Air

There are only two practical ways of arriving in Hawaii: by private boat, preferably a fine yacht, or, for most of us, by commercial flights.

International and US domestic flights arrive at and depart from the Honolulu International Airport, sometimes continuing on to neighboring islands. North American gateway cities include Los Angeles, San Francisco, Seattle and Vancouver. International gateway cities – primarily from Asia – include Tokyo, Taipei, Hong Kong, Manila and Sydney.

Making a transfer in Honolulu from an international/mainland flight to an interisland one is easy as both terminals are at the same airport but housed in separate buildings. Shuttle buses are available.

Note: If going to Waikiki, don't rent a car at the airport and drive. Take a taxi.

There is no direct and easy way from th airport to Waikiki. Pick up a rental ca in Waikiki. Also, don't plan on takin the public bus from Honolulu airport luggage cannot be brought on board.

TRAVEL ESSENTIALS

When To Visit

Anytime, of course. There are two peal tourist seasons: June through August and December through February. Reserva tions for peak times should be made ir advance.

Visas and Passports

Entry requirements and restrictions are exactly the same as for anywhere else ir the United States. Canadians don't require a passport.

Vaccinations

None needed. But forget your pet, as all animals must be quarantined for a minimum of four months on arrival in Hawaii.

Weather

There are two seasons: warm and less warm. It's warmest from April until November, but nearly-constant trade winds keep humidity down. August and September are the hottest, and sometimes humid. December through February is coolest but these are also the months when rain is the heaviest, although it rains nearly everyday somewhere on each island. Weather varies widely from island to island, and on an island itself. If it's rainy in one place, it's usually sunny somewhere else on the island.

Trade winds are usually from the north-ast. The windward side of an island – the northeast side – is wettest and greenst. Leeward sides, in the western rain shadow of mountains, are drier and sunnier. When the northeast trades stop, southerly winds often take over, called kona winds. Hot and humid weather follows; fortunately, kona winds are rare in summer.

Weather information: Tel: 833 2849.

Clothing

Casual and light, nearly always. No neckties, but a sports jacket is required at some restaurants. Bring a light jacket or sweater for cool winter evenings and higher elevations.

Electricity

Standard US 110–120 volt, 60 cycle AC.

Time Differences

Same day as mainland North America, one day behind Asia. Time is two hours behind Los Angeles, five hours behind New York, 10 hours behind London. Hawaii does not shift to summer daylight savings time.

GETTING ACQUAINTED

Geography

The Hawaiian Island chain extends 1,523 miles (2,437km) southeast to northwest, from the Big Island to Kure Atoll, near Midway. Don't make a common mistake: Hawaii is not in the South Pacific. Hawaii is above the equator, far north of Tahiti, and on the same latitude as Mexico City and Hong Kong. There are eight main islands, all in the chain's southeastern part: Hawaii (aka Big Island), Maui, Kahoolawe (uninhabited), Lanai, Molokai, Oahu, Kauai and Niihau. Two islands, Lanai and Niihau, are private and closed to visitors. Total land area is 6,425sq miles (16,640sq km), two thirds of that belonging to the Big Island.

Government and Economy

State executive powers are constitutionally vested in a governor and lieutenant governor, elected every four years. A bicameral legis-

lature meets yearly in Hawaii's capital, Honolulu. Hawaii's government exists only on two levels: state and county. There is one combined city and county jurisdiction, Honolulu, including Oahu and the islands not within the three other non-metropolitan jurisdictions, or counties, of Hawaii, Maui and Kauai.

Economically, the per capita buying

power in Hawaii is quite low; the cost of living is second highest in the United States. Sugar and pineapple were once modern Hawaii's economic base. Tourism is now number one, with 7 million visitors in 1990 bringing US$9.4 billion to Hawaii. The American military presence adds substantially to Hawaii's economy.

Religion

Catholic, Protestant, Mormon, Buddhist.

How Not to Offend

Easy: remember that Hawaii is neither a theme park nor a fantasy island. Rather, it is home for a million people, with their own life-styles and expectations. Don't judge people and life-styles by Western standards. Hawaii is more Asian and Pacific than American and European, a fact easily forgotten by visitors. Hawaii is friendly and gracious, but it runs on island time. Other suggestions:
• Don't try to speak or mimic the local English patois, usually called pidgin English. Only a true kama'aina can speak it properly. Visitors and newcomers trying to speak it sound ridiculous and even mocking.
• Don't ever honk your car's horn; it's considered terribly rude and unnecessary.

KAPU
NO FISHING

- Don't lean on old cars; it belongs to someone, and under that paint could be nothing but rust. You might put a hole in the car. No joke.
- Don't wear his-and-her matching Hawaiian shirts and/or muumuus. Actually, no one is offended by this, but you'll spare yourself some snickers.

Whom Do You Trust

Everybody. Honolulu, for example, is one of the safest cities in the United States. Most problems, when they occur, are with unattended rental cars at beach and lookout parking lots. Lock the car and don't leave valuables in view.

Population

Statewide: 1,108,229. About 80 percent reside on Oahu. Descending order of population: Caucasian, Japanese, Filipino, Chinese, Black, Korean, Hawaiian, Samoan and Puerto Rican.

MONEY MATTERS

Currency

Standard US currency and coins in all the usual denominations. $1=100 cents.

Credit Cards

All internationally-popular cards accepted: American Express, Visa, Master-Card, and to a lesser degree, Diners Club. Essential for car rental.

Cash Machines

Everywhere – at bank branches and shopping centers – and accessible 24hrs daily. Bank of Hawaii's machines are the most universal, accepting a range of cards.

Tipping

Yes, for food and drinks, taxis, baggage porters, and where you feel it's deserving. Ten to 20 percent, with 15 percent being the norm.

Money Changers

Banks and hotels, with hotels offering a lower exchange rate. Bank of Hawaii and First Hawaiian Bank have the most branches statewide. Street changers are nonexistent.

GETTING AROUND

Taxi

Airports and in Waikiki, not so commo elsewhere on Oahu and the neighborin islands. Don't expect to flag down one o the street. Use the telephone to summo one. Rates are metered, although for lon trips, a flat rate may be negotiated.

Bus

Only Oahu has a comprehensive bus sys tem, TheBus, and it is superb. Connec tions and frequency are excellent, an TheBus goes everywhere, including aroun the island. Flat fare one-way anywhere i US$1. For route or connection informa tion: tel: 848 5555.

Car

The only practical transportation in mos of Hawaii. Rates are among the cheapes in the world; competition is stiff, but b safe and book in advance. Weekly rate and air/hotel package rates are cheapes when booked in advance. Day rates wit unlimited miles are standard. Hawaiia and Aloha Airlines offer good deals o neighboring islands, sometimes even o an hour's notice off season. National com panies and locally-owned companies are on all main islands. Credit card required and an international driver's license often requested.

Right turns on red lights, after stopping, are okay.

Ferry

Nothing except the *Maui Princess*, plying between Maui and Molokai, and used mostly by commuting hotel employees. Unprotected and dangerous waters between islands make ferries impractical.

Inter-Island Flights

By commercial airlines, mostly by jet. Schedules are frequent and convenient, hourly on popular routes.

Flights average only half an hour in the air. But add time on both ends for rental car pick up and return, hotel check in and check out, ground travel time, and all those unexpected things that slow you down when rushed. I recommend budgeting four hours of total time.

The three main carriers are Aloha Airlines (and its subsidiary, IslandAir), Hawaiian Airlines and Mahalo Air. For reservations call:

Aloha Airlines
Oahu: Tel: 484 1111
Other islands: Tel: (800) 367 5250
Hawaiian Airlines
Oahu: Tel: 838 1555
Other islands: Tel: (800) 367 5320
Mahalo Air
Oahu: Tel: 833 5555
Other islands: Tel: (800) 462 4256

Disabled

Hawaii's visitor facilities are very good for those requiring special assistance. Most hotels offer facilities, including rooms, for those in wheelchairs. Request the *Aloha Guide for Persons with Disabilities* from the Commission on Persons with Disabilities, at 500 Ala Moana Blvd., Suite 210, Honolulu 96813. Tel: (808) 586 8121. Hawaii Visitors Bureau has a guide called *Aloha Guide to Accessibility*.

ACCOMMODATIONS
Hotels

There is a wide range of accommodations to suit all pockets and tastes. As with everywhere, the quality of the hotel is commensurate with price. Published rates for a double room (excluding the 9.25 percent room tax) are categorized as follows:
$ = under US$100, $$ = US$100–$150,

$$$ = over US$150. Make sure to ask for bargains, discounts, special room and car packages, and off season deals from travel agents and airlines.

Oahu

KAHALA MANDARIN ORIENTAL
5000 Kahala Avenue, Honolulu 96816
Tel: 734 2211 Fax: 737 2478
Toll: (800) 367 2525
Away from everything, but then not. Popular with statesmen and celebrities, it is casually exquisite and elegantly affluent. After a night, it feels like home. $$$

HALEKULANI HOTEL
2199 Kalia Road, Honolulu 96815, Waikiki
Tel: 923 2311 Fax: 922 5111
Toll: (800) 367 2343
Nobody disagrees: Waikiki's finest hotel. Mood and atmosphere seem independent of the Waikiki bustle despite prime location. Sophisticatedly discreet decor and staff. $$$

WAIKIKI PARC
2233 Helumoa Road, Honolulu 96815
Tel: 921 7272 Fax: 923 1336
Toll: (800) 422 0450
An affordable alternative to the Halekulani (same management). Back from the beach. An economical class act with the Halekulani's grace. Stunning ocean views higher up. $$

WAIKIKI JOY HOTEL
320 Lewers Street, Honolulu 96815
Tel: 923 2300 Fax: 924 4010
Toll: (800) 422 0450
Despite its name, popular for its upscale atmosphere and boutique size. Away from the beach and scenery, but pleasant. Out of the ordinary. $$

NEW OTANI KAIMANA BEACH HOTEL
2863 Kalakaua Avenue, Honolulu 96815
Edge of Waikiki
Tel: 923 1555 Fax: 922 9404
Toll: (800) 356 8264
Near Diamond Head and Kapiolani Park, away from central Waikiki. Known as a pleasant alternative to more expensive Waikiki hotels. Rooms are sometimes quite small, but nice. $$

MANOA VALLEY INN
2001 Vancouver Drive, Honolulu 96822
Manoa Valley
Tel: 947 6019 Fax: 946 6168
Toll: (800) 634 5115
Formerly the John Guild Inn, a 1920s mansion of 7 bedrooms. Above Waikiki in Manoa Valley, where it's quiet, cool, and a little more wet. $$

IHILANI RESORT & SPA
1001 Olani St, Kapolei 96707
West Oahu
Tel: 679 0079 Fax: 679 0080
Toll: (800) 626 4446
Blazing trails to west Oahu, this luxury resort has a neighboring island feel, glitzy multi-level spa, and a picture-perfect swimming cove. $$$

TURTLE BAY HILTON AND COUNTRY CLUB
57-091 Kamehameha Highway,
Kahuku 96731, North Shore
Tel: 293 8811 Fax: 293 9147
Toll: (800) HILTONS
Far from anywhere, with rugged views of the North Shore. A good retreat, whether for golf or for staring at the horizon. $$

Big Island

HAWAII NANILOA HOTEL
93 Banyan Drive, Hilo 96720
Tel: 969 3333 Fax: 969 6622
Toll: (800) 367 5360
This recently-refurbished and pleasant hotel on Banyan Drive is unquestionably Hilo's best choice. Great views of bay and Mauna Kea volcano. $$

MAUNA LANI BAY HOTEL & BUNGALOWS
1 Mauna Lani Drive,
Kohala Coast 96743
Tel: 885 6622 Fax: 885 4556
Toll: (800) 367 2323
Kohala's best, with less theatrics than its neighbors, and peerless service, ambience, and style. Ancient fishponds, petroglyphs, and other historical spots nearby. $$$

MAUNA KEA BEACH HOTEL
One Mauna Kea Beach Drive,
Kohala Coast 96743
Tel: 882 7222 Fax: 882 7552
Toll: (800) 882 6060

The original Big Island luxury resort, newly-renovated but still possessing it[s] original charm, a beautiful beach, an[d] museum-quality Asian and Pacific ar[t] throughout. $$$

THE ROYAL WAIKOLOAN
69-275 Waikoloa Beach Drive,
Waikoloa 96743
Tel: 885 6789 Fax: 885 7852
Toll: (800) 688 7444
It's impossible to be disappointed with this graceful and unpretentious hotel with a beautiful ocean front and ancien[t] Hawaiian fishponds. $$

KONA VILLAGE RESORT
P.O. Box 1299, Kailua-Kona 96745
North Kona
Tel: 325 5555 Fax: 325 5124
Toll: (800) 367 5290
Nothing else like it in Hawaii. Individual luxury *hales* with no telephones or TVs. No coats or ties permitted. Lose track of time and reality here. $$$

HOLUALOA INN
P.O. 222, Holualoa 96725, Near Kona
Tel: 324 1121 Fax: 324 1121
Perched in a small artists' town above Kona, this is a very quiet place of quality. Better than any typical bed-and-breakfast place. A fireplace, even. $$

ROYAL KONA RESORT
75-5852 Alii Drive, Kailua-Kona 96740
Tel: 329 3111 Fax: 329 9532
Toll: (800) 774 5662
Excellent location near downtown Kona, on the harbor. Sometimes busy, but with wonderful views and ambience. $$

MANAGO HOTEL
P.O. Box 145, Capt. Cook 96704
South Kona
Tel: 323 2642
An island classic, far from everything noisy and shiny. A friendly family-run place with a down-home restaurant and even a Japanese-style room. $

KILAUEA LODGE
P.O. Box 116, Volcano 96785
Tel: 967 7366 Fax: 967 7367

An estate built in the 1930s, it offers 11 rooms, several with fireplaces. Cool and quiet, with a classy restaurant popular island-wide. $$

Kauai

PRINCEVILLE HOTEL
P.O. Box 3069, Princeville 96722
North Shore
Tel: 826 9644 Fax: 826 1166
Toll: (800) 782 9488
Recently renovated, a no-holds-barred hotel of luxury with Hawaii's finest view. Indulge in both. One of Hawaii's friendliest hotel staffs. The soft smell of flowers everywhere. $$$

HANALEI COLONY RESORT
P.O. Box 206, Hanalei 96714
North Shore
Tel: 826 6235 Fax: 826 9893
Toll: (800) 628 3004
Better for families than recluses, comfortable but simple (no TVs) condo units are right on the beach. Last hotel on the road heading north. $$

HANALEI BAY RESORT
P.O. Box 220, Hanalei 96714
Tel: 826 6522 Fax: 826 6680
Tol: (800) 827 4427
Perched on a cliff, it offers the same north shore views as its neighbor, the Princeville Hotel, but at slightly lower prices. Units have kitchens. $$

KAUAI MARRIOTT RESORT & BEACH CLUB
Kalapaki Beach, Lihue 96766
Tel: 245 5050 Fax: 245 5049
Toll: (800) 228 9290
Formerly the Westin but less ostentatious than its predecessor. Horse-drawn carriages, lagoon boat tours, and Kauai's biggest swimming pool. $$$

HYATT REGENCY KAUAI
1571 Poipu Road, Koloa 96756
Tel: 742 1234 Fax: 742 1577
Toll: (800) 233 1234
The best and nicest in Poipu. Open-air courtyards, low-rise architecture and subdued elegance. Right on the beach. $$$

KOKE'E LODGE
P.O. Box 819 Waimea 96796
Koke'e/Waimea Canyon
Tel: 335 6061
A dozen simple but fully-equipped cabins in Koke'e State Park. Nothing but what's necessary. Popular and often booked. $

Maui

KAPALUA BAY HOTEL & VILLAS
1 Bay Drive, Lahaina 96761
West Maui
Tel: 669 5656 Fax: 669 4694
Toll: (800) 367 8000
Smooth and embracing, a Mediterranean-style place for hiding or golf. Classical music festival, wine symposium, lots of tranquility. $$$

WESTIN MAUI
2365 Ka'anapali Parkway, Lahaina 96761
West Maui
Tel: 667 2525 Fax: 661 5831
Toll: (800) 228 3000
Twelve acres of water, and more water. The Westin has set the Ka'anapali standard for elegance. Punctuated with Asian and Pacific art. $$$

MAUI MARRIOTT
100 Nohea Kai Drive, Lahaina 96761
West Maui
Tel: 667 1200 Fax: 661 8575
Toll: (800) 228 9290
Modest amidst the sparkle of nearby 'fantasy' resorts. Most rooms have ocean views. Comfortable, tasteful, and unpretentious. Friendly, relaxed staff. $$–$$$

LAHAINA HOTEL
127 Lahainaluna Road, Lahaina 96761
Tel: 661 0577 Fax: 667 9480
Toll: (800) 669 3444
Built in the 1860s, wonderfully restored with beautiful antiques and attention to detail. Near the waterfront. Romantic with cozy luxury. $$

THE PLANTATION INN
174 Lahainaluna Road, Lahaina 96761
Tel: 667 9225 Fax: 667 9293
Toll: (800) 433 6815
A new place but with plantation ambiance and details. A romantic and quiet alternative to the resorts, but with a modest swimming pool. $$

RENAISSANCE WAILEA BEACH RESORT
3550 Wailea Alanui Drive, Wailea 96753
Tel: 879 4900 Fax: 874 5370
Toll: (800) 992 4532
Consistently recognized for over a decade as one of the best. Lush, luxurious, personal but comprehensive. Romantic quiet beach. $$$

FOUR SEASONS RESORT
3900 Wailea Alanui, Wailea 96753
Tel: 874 8000 Fax: 874 2222
Toll: (800) 334 MAUI
Ocean views and attention to details everywhere. Princely luxury but so subdued, it never feels crowded or busy. $$$

HOTEL HANA-MAUI
P.O. Box 8, Hana 96713
Tel: 248 8211 Fax: 248 7202
Toll: (800) 321 HANA
The epitome of an exclusive hiding place (97 rooms), with large doses of luxurious Hawaiian atmosphere. And then there's the Hana Coast all around.... $$$

Molokai

COLONY'S KALUAKOI HOTEL & GOLF CLUB
P.O. Box 1977, Maunaloa 96770
Molokai
Tel: 552 2555 Fax: 552 2821
Toll: (800) 777 1700
Nestled on Molokai's west end, you get comfort and quiet in concert with the beautiful Kepuhi Beach. $$

Lanai

MANELE BAY HOTEL/LODGE AT KOELE
P.O. Box 774, Lanai City 96763
Lanai
Tel: 565 7700 Fax: 565 6744
Toll: (800) 321 4666
Lush, sensuous, Manele Bay is the tropical beach counterpart to the **Lodge at Koele** (same address, but located higher up in the hills). $$$

Bed & Breakfast

PACIFIC HAWAII BED & BREAKFAST
1312 Aulepe Street, Kailua 96734
Tel: 486 8838 Fax: 261 6573
Toll: (800) 999 6026

BED & BREAKFAST HONOLULu
3242 Kaohinani Drive, Honolulu 96817
Tel: 595 7533 Fax: 595 2030
Toll: (800) 288 4666

BED & BREAKFAST HAWAII
P.O. Box 449, Kapa'a 96746
Tel: 822 7771 Fax: 822 2723
Toll: (800) 733 1632

Condominiums

ASTON HOTELS AND RESORTS
2155 Kalakaua Avenue, Suite 500,
Honolulu 96815
Tel: 923 0745 Fax: 922 8785
Toll: (800) 922 7866
Call for information on its properties on the major Hawaiian islands.

HOURS AND HOLIDAYS

Business Hours

Hawaii wakes up early, and most people are in their offices by 8am. Offices hours are typically 8am to 5pm, Monday through Friday. Shopping centers open between 9.30am and 10am, closing around 9pm. Banks: 8.30am to 3pm, Monday to Thursday; until 6pm Fridays.

Public Holidays

Hawaii observes all US national holidays, plus two additional state holidays: Prince Kuhio Day on March 26, and Kamehameha Day on June 11.

USEFUL ADDRESSES

Hawaii Visitors Bureau (HVB)

Hawaii

Oahu, Waikiki: *Business Plaza, 8th Floor 2270 Kalakaua Ave, Honolulu 96815 Tel: 923 1811*
In the middle of Waikiki and with tons of information for the taking. Extremely efficient and helpful.
Big Island, Hilo: Tel: 961 5797
Big Island, Kailua-Kona: Tel: 329 7787
Kauai, Lihue: Tel: 245 3971
Maui, Kahului: Tel: 244 3530

North America

Canada
1260 Hornby Street, Suite 104 Vancouver, B.C. V6Z 1W2 Tel: (604) 669 6265

Los Angeles
Central Plaza, 3440 Wilshire Blvd Rm 610, Los Angeles CA 90010 Tel: (213) 385 5301

New York
350 Fifth Avenue, Suite 808 New York, NY 10118 Tel: (703) 691 1800

International

United Kingdom
P.O. Box 208 Sunbury on Thames Middx TW16 5RH Tel: (44 181) 941 4009 Fax: (44 181) 941 4011

Germany
Herzog HC GmbH, Borsigallee 17 60388 Frankfurt/Main Tel: (49 69) 42 089 089 Fax: (49 69) 41 25 25

Singapore
c/o World Express Pte. Ltd. 108, Middle Road #04-01 Bright Chambers Singapore 0718 Tel: (65) 221 8706 Fax: (65) 339 0015

HEALTH AND EMERGENCIES

Hygiene/General Health

The same standards as Europe and North America. Hawaii offers world-class medical care. Note that the United States doesn't have a national health plan; most hospital care is paid by private insurance or health plans. Tap water everywhere is safe. Don't drink stream or river water, even in the wilds.

Crime/Trouble

Hawaii is one of the safest places in the United States. As an urban center, Honolulu is exceptionally safe. Still, take the usual precautions as anywhere else. There can be problems at beach and lookout parking lots: rental cars stand out like intergalactic supernovas. Lock cars and don't leave valuables inside.

Police

Honest, professional and reliable. Can't be talked out of speeding tickets. Most officers use their own cars on neighbor islands and on Oahu outside of Waikiki. In other words, most police cars are unmarked and don't look like government-issued police cars, save for a very small single blue light on the roof. The radar is popular and widely used.

COMMUNICATIONS AND NEWS

Post

Domestic US rates apply within Hawaii and to the mainland; it costs the same to mail a letter within Honolulu as to New York. Domestic and international express mail service is available, as are most international courier services, including Federal Express, DHL and United Parcel.

Telephone

Area code for all islands is 808. Toll-free calls: dial 800, then the number. Inter-island calls are toll calls: dial 1-808 before the seven-digit number. To call abroad directly, first dial the international access code 011, followed by the country code: Australia (61); France (33); Germany (49); Japan (81); Netherlands (31); Spain (34); UK (44); US and Canada (1). If using a US credit phone card, dial the company's access number, followed by 01, then the country code. Sprint, tel: 10 333, AT&T, tel: 10 288.

Media

All major American broadcast and cable television networks are available. Several local stations broadcast programs in Japanese, Korean and other Asian languages. There are two statewide daily newspapers – the morning *Advertiser* and the afternoon *Star-Bulletin*. Neighboring islands have their own daily newspapers. Mainland newspapers are widely available at bookstores and large supermarkets.

USEFUL INFORMATION

Children

Children are welcome everywhere. Many of the larger hotels offer special programs and activities for children. Remember, however, that some high-end hotels are known for quiet and privacy, and noisy children may vanish without a trace.

Maps

Available most everywhere, especially bookstores. Best are the University of Hawaii Press maps, by James Bier (white cover with blue-and-green letters) and the Insight Pocket Map which comes with this guide. Also, all rental car companie offer free booklets with simple road map

LANGUAGE

English and Hawaiian are the official lan guages. English is the language of commerce, business, education, and nearly ev erything else. The exception is Niihau where Hawaiian is spoken. Also spoken are Japanese, Chinese, Korean, Samoan Vietnamese, and the local patois, called pidgin English

FURTHER READING

Atlas of Hawaii, by University of Hawaii The best reference book for informatior and maps covering nearly every aspect o Hawaii: geology, environment, social anc economic structure.

Hawaii's Birds, by the Hawaii Audubor Society. Bird watchers need this, as do those wondering what that pesky bird with the red head and gray body is.

Hawaiian Mythology, by Martha Beckwith. The unquestioned standard for decades. Good for a month of reading.

The Hula, by Jerry Hopkins and others. A fine introduction to Hawaii's traditional dance.

Mark Twain's Letters from Hawaii, by Mark Twain. Reprinted letters from when Twain was a newspaper correspondent.

Place Names of Hawaii, by Mary K. Pukui and others. This is the best guide to the meaning of Hawaiian place names.

Shoal of Time: A History of the Hawaiian Islands, by Gavan Daws. A superb book of Hawaii's history after Western contact.

Stories of Hawaii, by Jack London. Paperback reprint of this famous writer, who traveled in Hawaii in 1907.

Volcanoes in the Sea: The Geology of Hawaii, by Gordon A. MacDonald and others. The definitive book on the geological history of the Hawaiian islands.

Waikiki Beachboy, by Grady Timmons. A hardcover book covering the history and life-style of the beachboy.

Insight Guide: Hawaii, by Apa Publications, Hong Kong. Captures the exquisite beauty of the islands with insightful features and stunning photography.

Index

N, O

L, M

P

Q – U

W

ACKNOWLEDGMENTS

Cover	**Scott Rutherford**
Photography	**Scott Rutherford** and
Pages 10, 11	**Steve Wilkings**
14	**Jacques Drago, Don Severson Collection**
15	**John Webber, Don Severson Collection**
18	**Leonard Lueras**
21	**John Heaton**
Update Editor	**Marty Wentzel**
Cover Design	**Klaus Geisler**
Handwriting	**V. Barl**
Cartography	**Berndtson & Berndtson**